AF556980

MAJOR DEPRESSION
Prevention and Treatment

MAJOR DEPRESSION
Prevention and Treatment

By

MICHAEL R. LOWRY, M.D.
Assistant Professor of Psychiatry
The University of Utah
Salt Lake City, Utah

WARREN H. GREEN, INC.
St. Louis, Missouri, U.S.A.

Published by

WARREN H. GREEN, INC.
8356 Olive Blvd.
St. Louis, Missouri 63132 U.S.A.

ISBN No. 0-87527-186-3

Printed in the United States of America

PREFACE

Everyone experiences unhappiness on occasion. And the Psychology section of any reputable bookstore today contains a long list of books which suggest ways to overcome—even prevent—unhappiness. But unhappiness, or depressed mood, must be distinguished from Major Depression,* an illness which profoundly affects the lives of one of every five women and one of every ten men in our society at some time in their lives.

Among the greatest advances in modern Psychiatry have been the accurate description of Major Depression and the discovery of effective treatments for it. Both of these achievements will be discussed in detail in this book. Once Major Depression has been defined and effective treatments designed, attention becomes naturally directed toward its prevention.

Preventive strategies must be based upon a thorough knowledge of the etiology of depressive disorder. It is generally accepted that a number of factors—genetic, biological, psychological, and social—are involved in the etiology of Major Depression. However, the studies which identify these factors and papers which propose preventive strategies based upon knowledge of these factors are scattered widely throughout the professional literature and not readily available to the average reader. A first step toward prevention of Major Depression is a systematic critical review of the best scientific data available regarding the etiology of the disorder.

This book accordingly offers to the mental health professional (or, for that matter, the lay individual) interested in Major Depression a selective review of the current literature on its diagnosis, etiology, treatment, and prevention. Because the focus is on prevention and because knowledge of etiology is crucial to prevention, the discussion of data regarding etiologic factors is particularly detailed. For the

*"Depression," "depressive disorder," and "major depressive disorder" are used as synonyms for Major Depression in this text.

professional interested in research into the etiology of Major Depression (especially the relationship between life events and Major Depression), an ample discussion of pertinent methodological problems will be provided.

Our knowledge in these areas is rapidly expanding. No doubt this text will require substantial revision, based on new information, within the decade. At least we can hope so.

ACKNOWLEDGMENTS

If I have had a mentor in the development of this book and of my professional identity, it is George Winokur, M.D., Professor and Chairman of the Department of Psychiatry at the University of Iowa. For his insistence upon excellence in psychiatric diagnosis and the use of somatic therapies, and for his dedication to psychiatric research, my deepest appreciation.

I owe additional thanks to a list of secretaries, first and foremost Dianne Denneny, for their efforts in typing (and re-typing) various sections of this manuscript. And I must express my heartfelt gratitude to Lincoln D. Clark, M.D., for his generosity and accuracy in providing editorial review of the entire text. I hope the finished work reflects his contributions.

I would also like to thank my publisher, Warren H. Green, and my wife, Candace, for their patience and unfailing support during the writing of this book.

And, finally, I must acknowledge my parents, William and Muriel Lowry, who through nature and nurture, through love and encouragement, made me much of what I am, and thus this book what it is. To them I dedicate this work.

CONTENTS

MAJOR DEPRESSION
Prevention and Treatment

Chapter 1

PREVENTION OF PSYCHIATRIC DISORDERS

On February 17, 1977, President Jimmy Carter signed Executive Order #11973 establishing the President's Commission on Mental Health. It was the purpose of the Commission to review the mental health needs of our Nation and ultimately make recommendations to the President as to how those needs might best be met. The Commission performed a one-year fact-finding study, received information from many of the Nation's foremost mental health authorities, and submitted their recommendations in the *Report to the President from the President's Commission on Mental Health—Volume I* (1978).

The Commission concluded (among other things) that as a Nation we must during this decade "undertake a concerted national effort to prevent mental disabilities." The Commission further noted that new knowledge is of particular importance to such an undertaking; "not only is there no national strategy for prevention, there is no concerted effort to assess what is already known and to evaluate the effectiveness of promising approaches."

This text is the result of one man's effort to assess what is already known in the area of the prevention of one mental disability, i.e., depression, and to point to specific gaps in that knowledge which current and future research hold promise of filling. Only the results of such research will allow the unfolding of specific preventive approaches.

CATEGORIES OF PREVENTION*

Efforts to prevent any mental (or medical) disorder may be directed towards any or all of a number of points in the course of that disorder. Attempts to stop an illness before it starts fall into the category

*The following discussion borrows heavily on Leavell and Clark (1965).

of primary prevention. Primary prevention may be defined as reduction of the incidence (or occurrence) of new cases of a disorder in the population. Primary prevention may be seen as consisting of two essential aspects, i.e., the promotion of conditions that produce and reinforce health (e.g., mental health) and well-being, and the specific protection of individuals against the occurrence of specific disorders (e.g., depression). As a rule, specific protection against a disorder depends upon knowledge of the causes of the disorder, opportunity to apply that knowledge, and of course, the actual application of that knowledge.

Secondary prevention is defined as reduction of the duration of a disorder (after it has begun), and thus its prevalence (i.e., the number of persons in the population suffering from the disorder at any point, or during any period, of time). Secondary prevention depends upon the early diagnosis and successful treatment of a disorder which, in turn, depend upon the availability of reasonably accurate diagnostic methods, an alert and motivated public, and ample diagnostic and therapeutic facilities (Caplan, 1964).

Finally, tertiary prevention consists of limitation of the impairment due to a disorder after the disorder itself has ended. More simply, tertiary prevention consists of rehabilitation. While a disorder may leave residual defects, the individual's remaining capacities may be maximized so as to allow the individual to lead as full a life as possible. Tertiary prevention includes efforts to maintain contacts between the ill individual and his or her social networks, the avoidance of prolonged or repeated hospitalizations when possible, and broader social efforts to counteract the alienation or ostracism of ill individuals due to community prejudices (Caplan, 1964).

Depression (to be defined and described in detail in the next chapter) is, in the vast majority of cases, a self-limited disorder which leaves few, if any, residual defects in its wake. For this reason, the remainder of this text will focus on issues regarding primary and secondary prevention, omitting tertiary prevention from further consideration.

PRIMARY PREVENTION OF PSYCHIATRIC DISORDERS

No widespread disease is ever controlled by the treatment of affected individuals alone (i.e., secondary prevention), but only when its causes are identified and eliminated (i.e., primary prevention is employed) (Kessler and Albee, 1977). To reiterate, the specific protection of a population against a given psychiatric disorder depends upon an understanding of the cause, or etiology, of that disorder and, accordingly, the ability to identify individuals at high risk for the development of the disorder. Unfortunately our knowledge of etiology of the various mental disorders, including depression, remains incomplete, and our ability to identify individuals at high risk is at best limited. In the absence of such knowledge, psychiatry must depend on any of a number of conceptual models in developing preventive strategies.

CONCEPTUAL MODELS IN PSYCHIATRY*

Perhaps the most popular conceptual model in American psychiatry today is the medical model. The discussion thus far, and the approach of this text as a whole, are both based on principles from the public health discipline and reflect the use of this model. According to the medical model, psychiatric disorders (at least some psychiatric disorders) are conceptualized as medical illnesses, or diseases. Each disorder is presumed to have its own particular etiology (or causes) related to the anatomy, chemistry, and physiology of the brain. Each is recognized by the manifestation of particular signs and symptoms and their response to somatic treatment. Each is associated with its own course and prognosis.

As employed by public health workers, the medical model focuses attention on the characteristics of specific disease-producing stimuli or agents (for example, bacteria), those factors related to one's susceptibility or resistance to disease, and the interactions of these agents and host factors (i.e., the disease process). Once such information is available, preventive efforts can be aimed at eliminating disease-producing agents, strengthening host resistance, and/or preventing contact between agents and host.

The medical model has been successfully employed by public health professionals in eradicating a number of disorders with psychiatric symptoms, for example, general paresis (due to chronic syphilitic infection) and pellagra (due to vitamin B_3 deficiency). For each of these disorders, the biological etiology was identified and the associated agent or host factors systematically attacked. In contrast to such

*The following discussion borrows heavily on Lazare (1973).

"organic" diseases associated with or caused by structural or physiological changes in the involved organ, i.e., the brain, the vast majority of disorders managed by psychiatrists today are "functional" in nature, involving no currently known structural or physiological alterations in brain function related to etiology or outcome.

In any large group of patients complaining of depression, a thorough medical evaluation may discover a physical (or organic) basis for the symptoms of a few. Some may be suffering influenza or hepatitis which are producing their symptoms. Others may be suffering from thyroid dysfunction. Certainly such medical conditions must be sought and ruled out in the evaluation of any case of depressive disorder. However, no such organic basis is discovered even after the most thorough medical evaluation in the vast majority of depressed patients. They thus suffer a "functional" psychiatric disturbance.

Because so little is known about the etiology of most common psychiatric disorders today, it is argued by some that the medical model may be appropriate for secondary, but not primary, prevention of psychiatric disorders. Indeed, it may be true that there cannot be effective population-wide primary prevention of mental disabilities without the acceptance of psychological determinism, which holds that all behaviors (including manifestations of psychiatric disorders) are caused by antecedent interpersonal conditions and events (Kessler and Albee, 1977).

Psychological determinism is the main postulate of the psychological (or psychodynamic) model. According to this model, deprivations and distortions in interpersonal relationships early in life, particularly parent-child relationships, produce within an individual a certain vulnerability to the development of psychological symptoms in the presence of any of a number of stresses in adulthood. The type of symptoms which arise depend upon the nature and timing of the stresses confronted as an adult. Therapy is directed toward clarifying the psychological significance of remote and recent events; psychotherapy (as opposed to somatic therapy) is the primary treatment modality.

The third model, which also depends on psychotherapy as its primary treatment modality, is the behavioral model. The behavioral model is based on learning theory, and behavioral therapy based on models of classical and operant conditioning. According to the behavioral model, psychological distress is viewed as the result of maladaptive learning, and symptoms are seen as learned maladaptive behaviors which are maintained because they either produce positive effects or avoid negative ones. The symptoms themselves (rather than any underlying biological or psychodynamic aberration) are seen as the problems requiring solution, and the solution is accomplished through retraining the individual, i.e., reinforcing adaptive behaviors and extinguishing maladaptive ones.

A major shift in the field of behavioral therapy in the past decade has been toward a greater appreciation of the role of cognition in the causation and perpetuation of psychological, or psychiatic, disorders. Psychological symptoms, i.e., maladaptive feelings and behaviors, have come to be seen by many behavioral therapists as the result of internal stimuli, i.e., self-defeating self-verbalizations. A school of cognitive psychotherapy has been founded by individuals including, most prominently, A.T. Beck and Albert Ellis, upon the premise that altering such self-statements will ultimately alter the associated problematic feelings and behaviors. Beck and his associates have systematized their cognitive and behavioral interventions on the basis of learning principles and clinical experience and have specifically applied their techniques to the treatment of depressive disorder with some success (to be discussed further in Chapter 7).

The fourth conceptual model commonly employed in psychiatric diagnosis and treatment is the social model. This model focuses on the quantity and quality of the individual's relationships with the various social groups to which he or she belongs. Symptoms are regarded as an index of social disorder, and therapy is directed toward a restructuring of the relationships between the individual and his or her relevant social systems.

Such a classification of conceptual models is artificial in the sense that any one therapist will likely employ a combination of such models in the diagnosis and treatment of any given patient, and different combinations with different patients.

CRISIS INTERVENTION

The crisis intervention approach (as formulated by Gerald Caplan, 1964), the most widely renowned primary prevention program in psychiatry to date, represents a blending of the non-medical conceptual models. This approach is based upon a number of essential assumptions. First, it assumes that, in order to avoid eventual mental disorder, an individual requires a body of resources, of physical, psychosocial, and sociocultural supplies, commensurate with his or her stage of personality development. A crisis is defined as a situation which exposes an individual to demands which exceed his or her currently available resources. Such a crisis is viewed as both a potential turning point either toward or away from mental disorder and a time at which an individual is particularly susceptible to the influence of those about him. Finally, it is assumed that those about an individual in crisis can attempt to influence that individual, to prevent his or her succumbing to a mental disorder, in one of two ways. First, one may modify the individual's environment in order to either decrease the stress of the situation or to increase the supplies (support) available to the individual (per the social model previously discussed). Second, one may strive to strengthen the individual's competence and "coping" (problem-solving) skills to enable him or her to avoid and/or withstand the stresses involved now and, hopefully, in the future (per the behavioral model previously discussed).

The crisis intervention approach has been the subject of considerable criticism since its inception. First, the approach is nonspecific in both aims and methods. It aims toward preventing the development of mental disorder (i.e., any and all of the various mental disorders) in an individual (i.e., any and all individuals) in crisis (i.e., any and all situations which demand more than available supplies allow). But the specific kind and quantity of supplies required to enable an individual to avoid mental disorder at any given point in his or her development are not defined, and perhaps cannot be defined on other than a case-by-case basis (if then). But, how is one to know in any given situation whether or not the individual's supplies are adequate to meet the demands placed upon them? How is one to know which particular supplies need reinforcement? If shortages of particular supplies can be demonstrated to be associated with a higher incidence of mental disorder in the face of the stresses of adult life, how can one go about correcting these deficits in the individual in crisis? More importantly, how can society go about correcting these deficits among its members?

Taken to the extremes of its earliest and broadest possible application, crisis theory must advocate population-wide efforts to improve individuals' physical health (e.g., reduce poverty and pollution), to enhance individuals' psychosocial well-being (e.g., increase self-esteem and self-control), and to contribute to individuals' sociocultural supplies (e.g., teach child-rearing and interpersonal communication skills). Indeed, in such a light, any effort to better the human condition could be seen as aiding in the prevention of mental disorder (Kessler and Albee, 1977). Such efforts are certainly beyond the scope of the physician, or physicians as a group. They are the concerns of society as a whole.

Yet, I am unaware of any evidence to date that any such broad-based social welfare programs have any effect toward reducing psychopathology in any population. Nor have I been able to discover any clear evidence that interventions on behalf of individuals in crisis have succeeded in reducing the risk of their subsequently developing mental disorder.

Finally, the assumption that life circumstances lead to mental illness remains, despite repeated efforts to demonstrate its validity, unproven. In fact, evidence has mounted in recent decades on behalf of a large genetic contribution to at least the major mental disorders, including depression.

Theories formulated in an attempt to explain, and thus facilitate the prevention of, mental disorder as a whole have failed to demonstrate their usefulness. As one result of the application of the medical model to the field of psychiatry, a number of specific disorders (diseases, if you would), each with a clearly defined cluster of signs and symptoms, each with its own clearly defined course over time, each with its own clearly defined response to somatic treatment, have been delineated with some success. Depression is one such disorder. Future efforts toward preventing mental disorders must surely be suited to each such individual disorder, carefully tailored along the available lines of information regarding the genetic, biological, psychological, and social influences upon their development and/or successful treatment.

THE CHAPTERS TO FOLLOW

In the following chapters, I will attempt to review for you our current state of knowledge regarding depressive disorder and our potential to prevent it. We will explore the research pointing to a genetic basis for depressive disorder. While it is tempting to take the next step and speculate as to how these genetic influences may be translated into biochemical predispositions toward depressive disorder, I have purposefully chosen not to do so in this text. At this date, biochemical theories of the etiology of depressive disorder remain just that, i.e., theories. And none of these theories are without significant flaws. In any case, these theories and the research they have inspired are the subject of an ever-growing number of other texts (destined to be outdated by the time they reach their printing) available to the reader today.

After discussion of the genetics of depressive disorder, we will momentarily abandon the medical model in favor of the psychological model. We will, in Chapter 4, review the evidence which suggests that early life experiences—specifically one early life experience, i.e., the loss of a parent during childhood—predispose an individual to the development of depression during adulthood. Subsequently, in Chapter 5, we will review the literature associating life events (crises) with the onset of depressive episodes. In that chapter, the work of George W. Brown and associates in identifying the social origins of depression will be presented in some detail, and possible applications of the social model in the prevention of depression discussed.

Finally, we will return to the medical model and its application to the secondary prevention of depressive disorder. But are medical treatments, proven effective in terminating and preventing the recurrence of depressive episodes, secondary prevention by nature? If depressive illness is a trait (once manifest, chronic unto death), certainly all preventive measures initiated after its onset are secondary (or tertiary) in nature. However, if a depressive episode is (as I have stated and will state again) a time-limited state, prophylaxis against the recurrence of new episodes is primary prevention by nature, in the same sense that crisis intervention is primary (Spring and Zubin, 1977). In either case, we will briefly review the effectiveness of somatic therapies (drugs and electroconvulsive treatments) in terminating and preventing the recurrence of depressive episodes. And we will mention the current controversy regarding the place of psychotherapy in the treatment and prevention of mental depression.

In the next chapter, I will begin by defining depressive disorder as the term is to be used in the remainder of the text.

REFERENCES

Caplan, G.: *Principles of Preventive Psychiatry.* Basic Books, Inc., New York, 1964.

Kessler, M., and Albee, G.W.: An overview of the literature of primary prevention. In Albee, G.W., and Joffe, J.M., Eds., *Primary Prevention of Psychopathology, Volume I: The Issues,* pp. 351-399. University Press of New England, Hanover, New Hampshire, 1977.

Lazare, A.: Hidden conceptual models in clinical psychiatry. New England J. Med. 288: 345-351, 1973.

Leavell, H.R., and Clark, E.G.: *Preventive Medicine for the Doctor in His Community: An Epidemiologic Approach,* pp. 14–38. McGraw-Hill Book Company, New York, 1965.

President's Commission on Mental Health, The: *Report to the President from the President's Commission on Mental Health—Volume I.* U.S. Government Printing Office, Washington, D.C., 1978.

Spring, B., and Zubin, J.: Vulnerability to schizophrenic episodes and their prevention in adults. In Albee, G.W., and Joffe, J.M., Eds., *Primary Prevention of Psychopathology—Volume I: The Issues,* pp. 254-284. University Press of New England, Hanover, New Hampshire, 1977.

SUGGESTED FURTHER READING

Adler, D.A., Levinson, D.J., and Astrachan, B.M.: The concept of prevention in psychiatry: a re-examination. *Arch. Gen. Psychiat., 35:*786–789, 1978.

Bloom, B.L.: The logic and urgency of primary prevention. *Hospital and Community Psychiatry, 32:*839–843, 1981.

Erlenmeyer-Kimling, L.: Issues pertaining to prevention and intervention of genetic disorders affecting human behavior. In Albee, G.W., and Joffe, J.M., Eds., *Primary Prevention of Psychopathology—Volume I: The Issues,* pp. 68–91. University Press of New England, Hanover, New Hampshire, 1977.

Lamb, H.R., and Zusman, J.: Primary prevention in perspective. *Am. J. Psychiat., 136:*12–17, 1979.

Lamb, H.R., and Zusman, J.: A new look at primary prevention. *Hospital and Community Psychiatry, 32:*843–848, 1981.

Chapter 2

DEPRESSIVE DISORDER

In Chapter 1, we defined the three levels of prevention. It is now time to attempt to define the disorder we wish to prevent, i.e., depression.

"Depression" is a word with a multitude of meanings in our society today. It may be used to refer to a fleeting mood (i.e., sadness), to a sustained mood which may be one symptom of any of a number of illnesses, or to a complex clinical syndrome (or disorder) in which sadness—or something worse than sadness—is but one of several associated symptoms and signs. It is clear that many individuals experience a deep dejection qualitatively distinct from everyday sadness, a melancholia which assumes the dimensions of an illness—disruption of energy, sexual drive, appetite, and sleep, plus slowing of psychomotor functions, all with a reasonably predictable course, prognosis (including certain risks of morbidity and mortality), and response to somatic treatments. Throughout the remainder of this text, the terms "depression" and "depressive disorder" will be used interchangeably to refer to just such an illness.

RELIABILITY AND VALIDITY OF THE DIAGNOSIS OF DEPRESSIVE DISORDER

In 1970, Robins and Guze outlined five basic steps toward establishing the validity of any psychiatric diagnosis, i.e., toward formulating criteria which delineate a clinically meaningful disease entity. Their five basic steps are as follows:

1. *Clinical description*—The symptoms and signs of the disorder must be clearly defined, as must the disorder's relative prevalence among the different races and sexes, the usual age at

which the disorder has its onset, and any commonly associated precipitating factors.

2. *Laboratory studies*—The consistent association of reliable and reproducible laboratory (chemical, physiological, radiological, anatomical or even psychological) findings with a clinical syndrome goes a long way toward establishing its validity.
3. *Delimitation from other disorders*—Specific exclusion criteria (for example, disallowing the diagnosis of depressive disorder in any individual with demonstrated thyroid dysfunction) are essential to ensure the homogeneity of the specific disorder under consideration.
4. *Follow-up study*—If individuals with any given diagnosis are found, over the course of time, to demonstrate marked variation in outcome, particularly such variation as to lead to a change in diagnosis (e.g., from depressive disorder to schizophrenia) in a significant number of cases, the validity of the original diagnosis must be questioned.
5. *Family study*—If close relatives of individuals with a given disorder show an increased prevalence of that disorder when compared to the general population, the validity of that diagnosis is reinforced.

First, the clinical description of depressive disorder. A group of psychiatrists, headed by Robins and Guze at Washington University in St. Louis, developed rigorous criteria for the diagnosis of depressive disorder and 14 other psychiatric disorders, all of which they published in 1972 (Feighner *et al.,* 1972). The inter-rater reliability (the likelihood with which two different interviewers would come to the same diagnosis in evaluating any given patient) utilizing their criteria was reported to be very nearly 90%, an admirably high rate of reliability. Further, their criteria correctly predicted the follow-up psychiatric diagnosis in more than 90% of the cases among 314 outpatients (after 18 months' follow-up) and 87 inpatients (after 7 years' follow-up). Again an admirable track record.

These St. Louis, or Feighner, criteria were modified and elaborated to form the Research Diagnostic Criteria (RDC) (Spitzer *et al.,* 1977), which were developed as part of a collaborative project on the psychobiology of depressive disorders sponsored by the clinical research branch of the National Institute of Mental Health. The RDC for major depressive disorder have been included with only minor modification as the criteria for a depressive episode in the recently released Third Edition of the *Diagnostic and Statistical Manual* of the American Psychiatric Association (DSM–III).

To paraphrase DSM–III, a depressive episode is characterized first and foremost by a prominent and persistent dysphoric mood (e.g., sadness) or a pervasive loss of interest or pleasure in most usual activities. To qualify as a depressive disorder, this dysphoric mood or disinterest must represent a noticeable change in the individual's usual condition, must be of at least two weeks' duration, and must be associated with at least four of the following symptoms: decreased interest or pleasure in usual activities (or decreased sexual drive), diminished ability to think or concentrate (or make decisions), decreased energy, psychomotor agitation or retardation, a change in appetite or weight of 1 pound per week or 10 pounds per year (when not dieting), difficulty sleeping or sleeping too much, feelings of self-reproach or excessive guilt, and recurrent thoughts of death or suicide (or any suicidal behavior).

In addition to this symptomatic description, DSM–III provides specific exclusion criteria in order to delimit Major Depression from schizophrenia, from any mental disorder of demonstrated organic etiology, and from simple bereavement. (The reader is referred to DSM–III for further clinical description of Major Depression.)

Once a diagnosis of Major Depression is made on the basis of clinical history and interview, are laboratory tests available to confirm the diagnosis? Yes—for the first time—in the 1980's. For some time, it has been known that a substantial proportion (approximately one-half) of patients with unipolar depressive disorder manifest increased activity along the hypothalamic-pituitary-adrenal axis. These patients secrete larger than normal amounts of cortisol from their adrenals. And administration of dexamethasone fails to suppress their cortisol secretion (as it would in normal individuals). This dexamethasone suppression test (DST) identifies one-half of the patients clinically suspected of having a unipolar depression with considerable specificity, i.e., very few false-positive findings.

It has recently been discovered that an additional test of endocrine function may be useful in identifying depressed patients. Normal individuals respond to administration of protirelin (thyrotropin-releasing hormone, TRH) by releasing increased amounts of thyroid-stimulating hormone. In a substantial minority (approximately one-third) of patients with unipolar depression, this response is blunted. Again, there are few false-positive results.

Combining the DST and TRH tests results in considerable diagnostic confidence for confirming a diagnosis of major depressive disorder. In a study of 50 inpatients with unipolar depression reported by Gold *et al.* (1981), 84% of the patients were identified by abnormal results on one or both of these tests. Targum *et al.* (1982) reported similar findings.

Further, electroencephalograms (EEGs) have revealed several abnormalities in the brain wave patterns of depressed patients during sleep. Preliminary studies have shown that these sleep measurements may be used, alone or in combination with the neuroendocrine challenge tests described above, to confirm a diagnosis of depression with considerable accuracy.

While such tests are now available, they do entail certain inconvenience and expense, and are currently utilized almost exclusively in research centers. The diagnosis of depressive disorder remains largely a clinical diagnosis and, even without the aid of laboratory confirmation, a stable diagnosis over time.

In 1972, Robins and Guze reviewed all English-language reports of follow-up studies (involving a follow-up period of at least one year) of patients with mood disorder. These studies demonstrated a predictable outcome for depressive disorder, predictable clinical remission. Among the studies reviewed, depressive disorder developed into a chronic state in only 1–23% of the patients involved; in general, the longer the period of follow-up, the fewer the patients determined to be chronically ill. Further, a change in diagnosis from depressive disorder to schizophrenia occurred in only 2–7% of the cases reviewed.

PREVALENCE OF DEPRESSIVE DISORDER

Depressive disorder is a common illness in our society. Its precise prevalence in the American population is just now being determined by systematic studies. One recent survey of a U.S. community (New Haven, Connecticut), employing a structured interview designed to elicit psychiatric diagnoses according to the RDC, found a point prevalence of major depressive disorder (excluding grief, i.e., a depressive episode occurring within three months of the death of a close relative) of 4.3%—3.2% among men, 5.2% among women (Weissman and Myers, 1978). That same study (Weissman and Myers, 1978) estimated that 20% of the individuals in that community (12.3% of the men and 25.8% of the women) would develop a depressive disorder at some point in their lives. Based on these figures, one of every five Americans can expect to experience depression (as we have defined it) at some time in their lives. As many as one of every twenty-five may be depressed at this very moment.

CLASSIFICATION OF AFFECTIVE DISORDERS

In view of the large number of individuals suffering depressive disorder, it is a small wonder that psychiatrists have attempted to divide such a group into smaller, more homogeneous subgroups. Unfortunately, no such classification scheme has yet survived the tests of time and systematic study in order to gain universal acceptance.

Early in this century, depressive disorder (like all mental illness) was divided into neurotic and psychotic forms, largely as a result of the influence of psychoanalytic theory. Over the course of time, however, multiple definitions of the terms "neurotic" and "psychotic" have arisen. It has become impossible to know what a psychiatrist means when he describes a patient's depression as psychotic, as opposed to neurotic. Does he mean that the patient has lost contact with reality? Or that the patient has no insight into his or her illness? Or that the patient is so ill as to be incapacitated? Or that the patient is suffering delusions or hallucinations? Further, considerable controversy surrounds the issue as to whether neurotic depressions are simply the less severe, and psychotic the more severe, forms of the disorder. Such a quantitative subdivision of depressive disorders would obviously be of less clinical importance than a qualitative one.

A second, related attempt was made to divide depressions into those which were considered exogenous (i.e., precipitated by some life event) and those which were endogenous (i.e., without any obvious precipitant, and presumably of some biological etiology). Certainly, many patients with exogenous depression may also be viewed as neurotic, and many with endogenous depression might simultaneously be classified as psychotic. Yet, many "neurotic" depressions appear to arise in the absence of any particular precipitant, while many "psychotic" depressions immediately follow major life events.

But separating depressive episodes into exogenous and endogenous subgroups is not as easy as it initially appeared. Often patients attribute the onset of their depressions to events which cannot be shown to have occurred in fact, or which certainly would not precipitate an emotional response of such degree in most individuals. Even if a depressed individual has suffered some sort of crisis (for example, the loss of a job or the end of an important relationship), how is one to know whether the crisis caused the depression or the depression produced the crisis? The crisis can only be presumed to have precipitated the depressive disorder if it predated the onset of depressive symptoms. But retrospective dating of symptoms can be extremely difficult to do with any degree of accuracy. We will discuss such difficulties in further detail when we return to the topic of the association of depressive disorder with life events in Chapter 5.

Finally, experts in the field have attempted to separate depressive disorders into two groups, endogenous and reactive, on the basis of specific clusters of clinical symptoms. For example, endogenous depressives are typically characterized as suffering early morning awakening and feeling most depressed in the morning. On the other hand, reactive depressives classically suffer initial insomnia and feel worse in the evening. Attempts to subdivide large groups of depressed patients employing such symptomatic differences have met with some success (particularly when employing sophisticated statistical techniques such as factor analysis), but remain often difficult to apply to an individual patient, wherein they may be confounded by factors related to the severity of depression and/or the individual's premorbid personality traits.

Although classification schemes attempting to subtype depressive disorders according to presence or absence of either precipitants or certain clusters of depressive symptoms have not proven particularly useful, new schemes developed in the past two decades based on family studies of depressed patients are proving to be of some clinical relevance.

A small subgroup of depressed patients suffer not only depressive moodswings, but also occasional shifts in mood to the other extreme, i.e., mania. The manic patient experiences an elevated or expansive (or sometimes irritable) mood and a cluster of associated symptoms including at least four of the following (according to DSM–III): increased involvement in a variety of activities, failure to recognize the potential for adverse consequences of one's activities (e.g., reckless spending sprees), distractibility, decreased need for sleep, increased talkativeness, racing thoughts or flight of ideas, and grandiosity. These symptoms must represent a change from the individual's usual functioning and have lasted at least a week to qualify as a manic episode. Schizophrenia and organic mental disorder must be ruled out. A mood disorder manifested by moodswings to both high and low extremes, or poles, in a given patient is known as Bipolar Disorder. Patients who suffer one or more depressions, without ever suffering a manic episode, are said to suffer unipolar disorder.

Studies beginning in the mid 1960's have demonstrated that bipolar affective disorder differs significantly from unipolar affective disorder in a number of respects. Firstly, bipolar illness tends to cluster in families; relatives of bipolar patients suffer bipolar illness (and affective disorder, i.e., bipolar illness plus unipolar illness) significantly more often than do relatives of unipolar patients. Further, bipolar patients (in comparison to unipolar patients) have consistently been demonstrated to experience an earlier age of onset of their affective illness, to experience more episodes of illness, and to respond more frequently to treatment with lithium carbonate. Thus, the distinction between bipolar and the unipolar affective disorder is an important one with implications regarding genetic etiology, prognosis, and treatment.

The lifetime prevalence of bipolar illness is, however, only about 1.2% in both males and females (Weissman and Myers, 1978). The vast majority of depressed patients, therefore, are unipolar, and that large unipolar group of patients continues to be the subject of controversy as regards classification.

The reader may already have noted that one of the five steps toward establishing validity of the diagnosis of depressive disorder, i.e., family study of depressive disorder, has been avoided thus far in our discussion. In the next chapter, we will review the evidence from family studies of depressive disorder which suggest a genetic component to the etiology of the illness while simultaneously reinforcing its validity. We will also, in Chapter 3, review Winokur's proposal

(1973) that the group of unipolar depressive patients can be meaningfully subdivided on the basis of their family histories of psychiatric disorder.

REFERENCES

Feighner, J.P., Robins, E., Guze, S.B., Woodruff, R.A., Winokur, G., and Munoz, R.: Diagnostic criteria for use in psychiatric research. *Arch. Gen. Psychiat., 26:*57–63, 1972.

Gold, M.S., Pottash, A.L.C., Extein, I., and Sweeney, D.R.: Diagnosis of depression in the 1980's. *J.A.M.A., 245:*1562–1564, 1981.

Robins, E., and Guze, S.B.: Establishment of diagnostic validity in psychiatric illness: its application to schizophrenia. *Am. J. Psychiat., 126:*983–987, 1970.

Robins, E., and Guze, S.B.: Classification of affective disorders: the primary-secondary, the endogenous-reactive and the neurotic-psychotic concepts. In Williams, T.A., Katz, M.M., and Shield, J.A., Jr., Eds., *Recent Advances in the Psychobiology of the Depressive Illnesses,* pp. 283–293. U.S. Government Printing Office, Washington, D.C., 1972.

Spitzer, R.L., Endicott, J., and Robins, E.: *Research Diagnostic Criteria for a Selected Group of Functional Disorders,* Third Edition. Biometrics Research, New York State Psychiatric Institute, New York, 1977.

Targum, S.D., Sullivan, A.C., and Byrnes, S.M.: Neuroendocrine interrelationships in major depressive disorder. *Am. J. Psychiat., 139:*282–286, 1982.

Weissman, M.M., and Myers, J.K.: Affective disorders in a U.S. urban community. *Arch. Gen. Psychiat., 35:*1304–1311, 1978.

Winokur, G.: The types of affective disorders. *J. Nerv. Ment. Dis., 156:*82–96, 1973.

SUGGESTED FURTHER READING

Akiskal, H.S., and McKinney, W.T., Jr.: Overview of recent research in depression—integration of ten conceptual models into a comprehensive clinical frame. *Arch. Gen. Psychiat., 32:*285–305, 1975.

Gillin, J.C.: Sleep studies in affective illness: diagnostic, therapeutic, and pathophysiological implications. *Psychiatric Annals, 13:*367–384, 1983.

Hirschfeld, R.M.A., Koslow, S.H., and Kupfer, D.J.: The clinical utility of the dexamethasone suppression test in psychiatry: summary of a National Institute of Mental Health workshop. *J.A.M.A., 250:*2172–2177, 1983.

Mendels, J., and Cochrane, C.: The nosology of depression: the endogenous-reactive concept. *Am. J. Psychiat. 124:* Suppl. (May) 1–11, 1968.

Spitzer, R.L., Endicott, J., and Robins, E.: Research diagnostic criteria—rationale and reliability. *Arch. Gen. Psychiat., 35:*773–782, 1978.

Sternbach, H., Gerner, R.H., and Gwirtsman, H.E.: The thyrotropin releasing hormone stimulation test: a review. *J. Clin. Psychiat., 43:*4–6, 1982.

Targum, S.D.: Neuroendocrine challenge studies in clinical psychiatry. *Psychiatric Annals, 13:*385–395, 1983.

Chapter 3

EVIDENCE FOR A GENETIC BASIS OF DEPRESSIVE DISORDER

Five criteria may be listed which suggest the presence of a genetic factor in any illness of unknown etiology. These are as follows:

1. A rate of occurrence of the same disorder among relatives of ill individuals (i.e., probands) which is greater than the rate of occurrence of the disorder in the general population.
2. An excess of defects (or disorders) affecting the same functional system (e.g., the brain) among relatives of probands.
3. A higher concordance rate* among monozygotic (identical) as opposed to dizygotic (fraternal) twins.
4. A concordance rate among monozygotic twins reared apart which is similar to the concordance rate among monozygotic twins reared together.
5. A higher frequency of illness among probands' (ill individuals') children adopted away at birth than among well individuals' children adopted away at birth.

Each of these criteria will be explained in greater detail in the discussion which follows. It may be noted at this point that, while all of the criteria point to a familial background for a disorder, only the last two criteria point particularly to a genetic (as opposed to an environmental) etiology of the illness.

EVIDENCE FROM FAMILY STUDIES

As noted in the previous chapter, the validity of any psychiatric diagnosis is reinforced if and when it is demonstrated that relatives of

*A concordance rate is an expression of the frequency with which both members of a pair of twins will be found to suffer the same disorder (given one member has the disorder to begin with).

individuals with the disorder suffer the disorder more frequently than do individuals in the general population. An increased incidence of related disorders (defects in the same functional system) among probands' relatives offers additional supportive, though less direct, evidence along these lines.

As part of the "Iowa 500" study conducted over the past several years in the Department of Psychiatry of the University of Iowa School of Medicine, investigators interviewed 413 first-degree relatives (i.e., parents, siblings, and children) of patients with unipolar depressive disorder plus 415 relatives of patients with various medical illnesses. It should be noted that investigators did not know whether the index patients (probands) suffered depression or medical illness; the investigators were "blind" to the initial diagnosis in each case. The investigators discovered that 9.4% of the first-degree relatives of unipolar patients themselves suffered depressive disorder, compared to only 5.5% of the relatives of the medically ill control patients—a difference which was statistically significant (Winokur, 1979). This large-scale study thus demonstrates an increased incidence of depressive disorder among relatives of depressed patients when compared to the relatives of medically ill patients (representatives of the general population).

Numerous other studies have further demonstrated an increased incidence of both alcoholism and antisocial personality disorder among the brothers of unipolar depressive patients (when compared to the brothers of normal controls) and, conversely, an increased incidence of unipolar depressive disorder among the siblings of alcoholic patients. Thus, there appears to be an excess of related psychiatric disorders (i.e., alcoholism and antisocial personality) among the relatives of depressed individuals—further evidence in favor of the validity of the diagnosis and a familial basis for the disorder.

Finally, as already noted in Chapter 2, bipolar patients have been demonstrated to have an even greater familial loading of affective disorder than unipolar patients. Again, bipolar illness itself clusters in families, with relatives of bipolar patients suffering bipolar affective disorder significantly more often than the relatives of unipolar patients. Further, the overall risk of affective disorder (bipolar and unipolar disorders combined) is greater among relatives of bipolar probands than unipolar probands.

EVIDENCE FROM TWIN STUDIES

Monozygotic twins are identical with regard to their genetic make-up, while dizygotic (fraternal) twins have only half of their genetic material in common (as do other siblings). Since identical twins share a larger portion of their genes, evidence that a larger proportion of monozygotic (as opposed to dizygotic) twins share the same psychiatric disorder in their lifetime is consistent with, and perhaps suggestive of, a genetic basis for the disorder. Further, since fraternal twins have the same amount (50%) of genetic material in common as do other siblings, fraternal (dizygotic) twins should share a genetically caused disorder no more often than do other siblings.

In 1976, Allen analyzed all major studies (completed to that date) of sets of twins which included at least one member who suffered affective disorder. His figures showed, for bipolar illness, a monozygotic concordance rate of 72%; 60 of 83 sets of twins studied were concordant in that both members were shown to suffer bipolar illness. In contrast, only 14% (31 of 226 sets) of the dizygotic twins were concordant. This difference was highly significant statistically ($p < 0.001$). Similarly, with regard to unipolar depressive disorder, monozygotic concordance was 40% (6 of 15 sets of twins) compared to a dizygotic concordance rate of only 11% (4 of 36 sets). This difference was again statistically significant (Allen, 1976). And, it may be noted that the 11% concordance rate for unipolar depressive disorder among dizygotic twins is essentially identical to the 9.4% frequency of illness among other first-degree relatives determined by Winokur (1979).

These data suggest a familial basis for mood disorders, the evidence for bipolar illness being somewhat stronger than that for unipolar depression. To accept these figures as evidence of a genetic etiology of affective disorder, however, one must assume that the environments of two identical twins during their upbringing are at least as different as are the environments of two fraternal twins.

This may be an erroneous assumption. It is conceivable that the higher concordance among monozygotic twins is due, at least in part, to their being raised under more similar environmental conditions than are dizygotic twins. Thus, the evidence from such studies is strongly suggestive, but not conclusive, of a genetic basis for depressive disorder.

EVIDENCE FROM STUDIES OF TWINS REARED APART

One way to eliminate the potential confounding influence of environmental factors in the upbringing of identical (versus fraternal) twins is to study monozygotic twins who were separated early in life and subsequently reared apart. It would seem reasonable to assume under these circumstances that the surroundings for such a set of monozygotic twins during early life would be at least as different as the surroundings of two fraternal (dizygotic) twins reared together. Thus, a high concordance rate among monozygotic twins reared apart indeed suggests a genetic basis for a disorder; a concordance rate among monozygotic twins reared apart which is as high as the concordance rate among monozygotic twins reared together is particularly convincing evidence along these lines.

In 1968, Price gathered together information regarding 12 pairs of monozygotic twins, each pair separated early in life and subsequently reared apart, and each pair including at least one member known to suffer a major mood disorder.

Three of the pairs were considered bipolar by Price; two of the index cases, or probands, suffered bipolar affective disorder, and the other, who suffered depression, had a bipolar father. These three pairs were 100% concordant for bipolar illness—in each of the three cases, the twin (reared apart from the index individual) manifested bipolar illness.

Of Price's 9 unipolar pairs, 44% were concordant—a figure essentially identical to Allen's figure of 40% for monozygotic twins reared together.

Such evidence is strongly suggestive of a genetic component in the etiology of mood disorders (again, especially bipolar mood disorders). Yet, let me offer one last word of caution. To accept these data as convincing, one must assume that these figures will remain constant as more and more sets of reared-apart monozygotic twins (identified by at least one mood-disordered member) are collected and added to their numbers. Such will not necessarily be the case. If one is seeking such sets of twins, identified by the presence of at least one depressed or manic member, it is only reasonable to assume that sets in which both members are ill will be more readily identified and reported. Higher concordance rates may, therefore, simply reflect the greater likelihood of discovery of concordant (as opposed to discordant) pairs of twins. But, another method—adoption studies—circumvents this difficulty and provides perhaps the most convincing evidence of a genetic basis of mood disorders.

EVIDENCE FROM ADOPTION STUDIES

Two adoption studies offer evidence of a genetic basis for affective disorder. In the first study, by Mendlewicz and Rainer (1977), the authors selected a group of adoptees with bipolar illness and then compared their adoptive parents versus their biological parents as to the incidence of psychiatric disorder in those two groups. They discovered that the biological parents (as opposed to the adoptive parents) manifested significantly greater affective disorder and significantly greater total psychopathology.

Cadoret (1978) used a somewhat different approach. He studied a large group of individuals (126 in all) who had been adopted away at birth and separated them into two groups, those with evidence of psychopathology in one or both of their biological parents (83 adoptees) and those without such evidence (43 adoptees). Of the 83 adoptees with at least one biological parent known to be psychologically disturbed, 8 had a parent (invariably the mother) with unipolar affective disorder. Of those 8 adoptees, 3 adoptees themselves suffered unipolar depression. Of the remaining 75 adoptees who had at least one biological parent known to suffer some other form of psychopathology, 4 of the adoptees had unipolar affective disorder. In addition, 4 of the 43 control adoptees (with no evidence of psychopathology in either biological parent) also had unipolar affective disorder.

Thus, 3 of 8 adoptees whose biological mothers were known to suffer unipolar depression themselves suffered unipolar depression, while only 8 of 118 adoptees whose biological parents suffered other psychopathology or no psychopathology suffered unipolar illness; this difference is highly significant statistically ($p < 0.002$) and points to a genetic component to the disorder.

In summary, if one takes bipolar patients who have been adopted away from their biological parents at birth and raised by adoptive parents, and one then looks for affective disorder (or other psychopathology) among the biological (as opposed to the adoptive) parents, more affective disorder and greater total psychopathology is found in those parents biologically (and genetically) related to the bipolar probands. Conversely, if one looks among the records of a large group of adoptees for evidence of unipolar affective disorder (as opposed to other psychopathology or no pathology at all) among their biological parents, and one then compares the incidence of unipolar depression among the adoptees with and without a depressed parent, one finds significantly more unipolar affective disorder among the adopted-away offspring of individuals with unipolar affective disorder than among the adopted-away offspring of individuals with other (or no) psychopathology. Evidence from both studies points to a link between the appearance of affective disorder in adoptees and the occurrence of affective disorder in their biological parents, who presumably have had little or no influence on the environments in which they were raised; the link may thus be assumed to be genetic, as opposed to environmental ("nature," not "nurture").

EVIDENCE FROM LINKAGE STUDIES

Linkage occurs when two genes (or, more accurately, loci), each responsible for a different trait, are located on the same chromosome, and close enough to one another on that chromosome that they assort (during reproductive subdivisions) together in a dependent fashion, i.e., that they stay "linked" together from one generation to the next. If a disorder of unknown etiology could be demonstrated to consistently assort (from generation to generation) in such a dependent fashion with some other trait for which the genetic locus has been identified, a genetic basis (and even a chromosome location) for that disorder would be convincingly shown.

Numerous studies (for example, a recent study by Mendlewicz *et al.*, 1979) have shown bipolar affective disorder to assort in a dependent fashion with an X-chromosome-linked form of color-blindness in a large number of family pedigrees. These studies, taken as a group, provide convincing evidence for the presence of an X-linked form of bipolar illness. At the same time, several reports from similar investigations have failed to demonstrate linkage between Bipolar Disorder and X-linked color-blindness. It would thus appear that Bipolar Disorder is genetically heterogeneous, i.e., that there must exist more than one means of inheritance of bipolar illness.

While studies of family pedigrees have thus demonstrated a likely mode of inheritance (i.e., X-linkage) for a subgroup of patients with Bipolar Disorder, pedigree studies of unipolar patients have thus far failed to convincingly demonstrate a specific mode of inheritance for that illness. The difficulty in identifying a specific mode of inheritance for unipolar depression may be presumed to be due to the fact that unipolar affective disorder is not a single disorder (in terms of its inheritance), but rather consists of a heterogeneous group of disorders with different forms of genetic transmission (perhaps including a subgroup of depressed individuals with no genetic basis for their disorder whatsoever). Further findings in this regard may have to await a subclassification of unipolar disorders of clinical (and genetic) relevance. Winokur (1979) has suggested such a division of depressive disorders, and preliminary data indicate that one of his depressive subgroups may indeed be linked to known genetic markers.

FAMILIAL SUBTYPES OF UNIPOLAR DISORDER

Winokur (1979) has suggested the following subdivision of unipolar disorders, according to the depressed individual's familial constellation of psychiatric disorder(s):

> depression spectrum disease—depression in an individual with a first-degree family member (parent, sibling, or child) known to suffer alcoholism or antisocial personality disorder;
>
> familiar pure depressive disease—depression in an individual with a first-degree family member known to suffer depression, and no history of alcoholism or antisocial personality disorder among first-degree family members;
>
> sporadic depressive disease—depression in an individual who has no history of depression, alcoholism, or antisocial personality disorder in any first-degree relative.

The above three subgroups each consist of individuals with Major Depression, and thus are symptomatically very similar. They do, however, differ significantly in certain important clinical respects. For example, patients with sporadic depressive disease have a later age of onset of their disorder than patients in either of the other two groups. Further, individuals with familial pure depressive disease appear to suffer more depressive episodes than either of the other two subgroups (Winokur, 1979).

A recent report from Winokur's group (Schlesser *et al.,* 1979) provides intriguing evidence which suggests that the genetic subtypes they have defined may also be separated by distinct pathophysiologies. The dexamethasone suppression test (discussed in Chapter 2) quite accurately distinguishes Winokur's genetic subtypes of depressive disorder, according to their recent report; 82% (23 of 28) of the patients with familial pure depressive disease were non-suppressors, compared to only 4% (1 of 23) of the depression spectrum disease patients, while the sporadic depressive disease group exhibited intermediate results (37%, or 13 of the 35 individuals failing to suppress normally) (Schlesser *et al.,* 1979). Thus, those individuals with familial pure depressive disease almost invariably failed to suppress (manifesting a disturbance of the normal activity of the hypothalamic-pituitary-adrenal axis), while patients with depression spectrum disease almost invariably exhibited normal hypothalamic-pituitary-adrenal function. The sporadic depressive disease group appears heterogeneous as regards their pathophysiology, and further delineation of this group would appear in order.

Finally, preliminary data from Winokur's group also indicate that depression spectrum disease may be linked, genetically, to such markers as C3 or alpha-haptoglobin (Winokur, 1979).

CONCLUSION

The evidence for a genetic component in the etiology of depressive disorder is persuasive. Yet, with the exception of a relatively few families in which bipolar affective disorder appears to be transmitted in an X-linked fashion, the exact mode of transmission of the disorder from one generation to the next has not been identified and cannot be predicted in any given family. Thus, counseling of families in order to prevent the transmission of depressive disorder from one generation to the next must rely largely upon empirical risk factors (e.g., the likelihood that a child will develop depressive disorder, given that one parent is known to suffer depressive disorder). The limits of genetic counseling for such families will be discussed in Chapter 6.

Further, given the fact that 40% of identical twins are concordant for unipolar depressive disorder (Allen, 1976), 60% are discordant; in the majority of sets of twins in which one member suffers depression, the other will not. This fact alone speaks to the importance of the environment in the etiology of depressive disorder. Speculations as to environmental predisposition and/or precipitation of depressive episodes will be explored in the next two chapters.

REFERENCES

Allen, M.G.: Twin studies of affective illness. *Arch. Gen. Psychiat., 33*:1476–1478, 1976.

Cadoret, R.J.: Evidence for genetic inheritance of primary affective disorder in adoptees. *Am. J. Psychiat., 135*:463–466, 1978.

Mendlewicz, J., Linkowski, P., Guroff, J.J., and VanPraag, H.M.: Color blindness linkage to bipolar manic-depressive illness. *Arch. Gen. Psychiat., 36*:1442–1447, 1979.

Mendlewicz, J., and Rainer, J.D.: Adoption study supporting genetic transmission in manic-depressive illness. *Nature, 268*: 327–329, 1977.

Price, J.: The genetics of depressive behaviour. In Coppen, A., and Walk, A., Eds., *Recent Developments in Affective Disorders: A Symposium,* pp. 37–54. British Journal of Psychiatry Special Publication No. 2, Headley Brothers Ltd., Ashford, Kent, England, 1968.

Schlesser, M.A., Winokur, G., and Sherman, B.M.: Genetic subtypes of unipolar primary depressive illness distinguished by hypothalamic-pituitary-adrenal axis activity. *Lancet 1*:739–741, 1979.

Winokur, G.: Unipolar depression—is it divisible into autonomous subtypes? *Arch. Gen. Psychiat., 36*:47–52, 1979.

SUGGESTED FURTHER READING

Gershon, E.S., Bunney, W.E., Jr., Leckman, J.F., Van Eerdewegh, M., and DeBauche, B.A.: The inheritance of affective disorders: a review of data and of hypotheses. *Behav. Genetics, 6*:227–260, 1976.

Lewis, D.A., Kathol, R.G., Sherman, B.M., Winokur, G., and Schlesser, M.A.: Differentiation of depressive subtypes by insulin insensitivity in the recovered phase. *Arch. Gen. Psychiat., 40*:167–170, 1983.

Chapter 4

CHILDHOOD BEREAVEMENT AND DEPRESSIVE DISORDER IN ADULTS

For ages, man has held childhood experiences to be crucial to personality development. Virgil is recorded as having remarked, in the century before Christ, that, "As the twig is bent the tree inclines." In this century, Freudian theory has expanded upon this common-sense notion, outlining a series of stages of childhood development and a number of experiences necessary to allow a child to progress "normally" from one stage to the next and, ultimately, to adulthood. According to that theory, adverse experiences during childhood may contribute to abnormal personality development in some individuals, and to neuroses or psychoses (such as depressive disorder) in others; the exact adult outcome of any specific childhood experience is dependent upon the nature of the experience, the point in the child's development at which the experience occurs, and, potentially, a host of other factors (and is thus difficult, if not impossible, to predict). As regards depressive disorder, Abraham (1942) developed a theory that children who have suffered particular trauma or loss are subject to a condition he called "primal parathymia," which makes them more liable than others to develop melancholia in later life.

It is, however, one thing to develop a theory that appears to make sense and another to prove it. Early studies by a number of researchers attempting to verify the existence of an association between various forms of childhood deprivation and subsequent psychopathology in adulthood were gravely flawed and thus invalidated by a number of defects in methodological design (summarized by Gregory, 1958).

One of the great difficulties in doing research in the area is the impracticality of prospective study. Ideally, one might select for study a group of children who have undergone any of a number of adverse experiences in early life and follow them closely (noting the occurrence of additional adverse events along the way) well into adulthood in order to determine the influences of their earlier experiences upon the development of psychiatric disorders in adult life. The demands of time (both investigators' and subjects') and money required by such a study, however, are prohibitive. Thus, most research regarding the association of childhood experiences and subsequent psychological disturbance have begun by selecting a group of adults with one or another psychiatric disorder and seeking in their histories evidence of trauma in childhood.

In the past two decades, a number of investigators have focused their efforts on finding a history of childhood bereavement (particularly, loss of a parent during childhood) in adult patients with depressive disorder. Childhood bereavement has been selected for study because, compared to other sources of childhood deprivation (e.g., parental separation), its occurrence is unlikely to be unknown to, or denied by, the adult subject and can often be verified by other sources; childhood bereavement can be identified with a high degree of reliability.

Further, it is a quantifiable event which is subjectable to statistical analysis. Finally, while other forms of deprivation (e.g., parental separation) might lead one to suspect the presence of psychiatric disorder such as alcoholism or antisocial personality disorder in the parents (i.e., a genetic etiology), parental death (excepting suicide) may be assumed to be independent of the behavioral pattern of the family and thus to represent a largely environmental influence.

It is hypothesized by most investigators in the field that depressive illness in adulthood is the result of the reactivation (through, possibly, minor rejections) of a yet unresolved grief reaction to the loss of a parent during childhood—like an anaphylactic reaction in adulthood, as it were, when there has been sensitization in childhood. If such an hypothesis were indeed validated, it would have important implications for the prevention of depressive disorder. It would suggest that children who have lost a parent deserve particular attention—assistance, for example, in completing the process of grieving and/or compensation for their loss via an adequate emotional attachment to a parent substitute—in order to prevent the subsequent development of depressive disorder during adult life. Unfortunately, even the most recent research in this regard continues to be plagued by methodological problems. Let me mention a few.

In order to associate childhood bereavement with depressive disorder, one must first be able to clearly define depressive disorder. In the past few decades, various definitions of this disorder have been employed by the various investigators involved. The definitions, if reported at all in the relevant studies, differ from study to study, making comparisons between studies or the accumulation of evidence over the course of a number of studies difficult if not impossible. Even in those studies which list specific criteria for the diagnosis of depression, patients with secondary depression (i.e., depressive disorder arising in an individual with another, pre-existing psychiatric disorder) are rarely separated from those with primary depressive disorder (i.e., affective disorder which predates any other psychiatric disorders in the individual under study). If patients with secondary depressive disorder are not excluded from consideration, one cannot determine whether childhood bereavement is associated specifically with depressive disorder or whether it may be associated with the subjects' other pre-existing disorders, or with psychiatric disorders in general. Studies limited to individuals with primary depressive disorder (preferably without any other secondary psychiatric disorder) would offer much more conclusive evidence as to the specific association of childhood bereavement with adult depressive disorder.

The incidence of childhood bereavement in any population is dependent upon a variety of variables, including the geographic location of the population, the ages of the subjects, the ages of the subjects' parents at the time of the subjects' birth, and, finally, the social class of the subjects' parents. Studies comparing the incidence of childhood bereavement in samples of depressed individuals versus various control groups rarely match the experimental and control groups on most, let alone all, of these variables—never for the social class of the parents. Thus the depressive groups under study are not only inconsistently identified in these reports but also inadequately matched with control groups with respect to a number of essential variables.

The final problem I will mention is related to the retrospective nature of these studies. A number of the studies consist of reviews of patient records (rather than interviews with patients themselves) and select for study only those records containing adequate information regarding parental deaths. Such a selection procedure produces an inherent bias in that inadequate records which are discarded may well include a higher frequency of parental death during childhood than do adequate records. A record may contain no mention of the existence of a parent for the very reason that the parent died during the patient's childhood.

In the remainder of this chapter, I will attempt to review the research of the past 20 years (despite its limitations) regarding the association of childhood bereavement and adult depressive disorder. Such an attempt is rarely undertaken elsewhere in the literature. Some no doubt would hold that research flawed by the deficiencies already noted does not merit detailed review. Others seem already convinced, by one or another of the studies to be reviewed, that the question has already been successfully answered and that there is no further need for discussion. Still others, no doubt, attempt some synthesis of the available evidence and become so confused in so doing that they abandon their efforts in dismay.

I must admit my own dismay in attempting to make sense of these studies, compensating the weakness of one study with the strength of another, trying to reconcile disparate findings of apparently similar investigations, etc. Yet, I believe the effort must be made and am hopeful that the presentation of its results in this chapter will be of some merit, in particular to those who will pursue research in this area, enabling them to avoid at least some of the pitfalls which have plagued their predecessors.

I would encourage the reader to take this rather lengthy introduction as a warning. The ensuing review is guaranteed to be complex and at times confusing and frankly of less than universal interest. Accordingly, some may wish to proceed to the brief discussion at the end of this chapter wherein I will offer the few conclusions which research currently allows.

STUDIES COMPARING DEPRESSED PATIENTS WITH THE GENERAL POPULATION

A study by Felix Brown (1961) is perhaps most often quoted as providing evidence for an association between childhood bereavement and depressive disorder in adults. Brown studied a group of patients who had been referred by their general practitioners to the Outpatient Department of Hampstead General Hospital in London for evaluation of depressive symptoms. Brown employed Sir Aubrey Lewis' definition of depressive illness as an illness in which the clinical picture is dominated by persistent unpleasant affect, without schizophrenia and without organic brain disease. He studied all of the patients in that outpatient clinic who suffered depressive illness (so defined) and about whom adequate records were available—a total of 216 patients. As one set of controls, Brown employed figures taken from the table on orphanhood of the 1921 census of England and Wales, a total population survey, and the only census figures on orphanhood available at that time.

Brown found that 41% of his depressed group of patients had lost a parent (by death) before age 15, compared to only a 16.6% frequency of childhood bereavement in the general population (as calculated from 1921 census data). Needless to say, the difference was highly significant. On the basis of a detailed evaluation of his findings, Brown drew a number of additional conclusions. Loss of the parent of the same sex appeared just as significant (i.e., equally associated with later depression) as loss of the parent of the opposite sex. And, when Brown divided the period of childhood (i.e., the period prior to the 15th birthday) into three equal time spans (i.e., birth to the 5th birthday, the 5th to the 10th birthday, and the 10th to the 15th birthday), the loss of a father appeared to be more significant in later childhood, i.e., at ages 5 to 14, whereas loss of a mother appeared equally significant in each of the 5-year periods. (Loss of either parent occurred significantly more often among depressives than among the normal controls for each of the three periods of childhood.) Brown's findings contradicted earlier theoretical assumptions that loss of a mother before age 5 would be the most significant factor in the later development of emotional problems, including depression.

Brown's study has been criticized for a variety of reasons, including his use of the 1921 census figures. The most profound defect in the study, however, in twenty years' hindsight, is its vague definition of depressive illness, a definition which lends itself to inconsistency and over-inclusiveness.

The importance of employing explicit diagnostic criteria is emphasized by a later study by Hopkinson and Reed (1966). Hopkinson and

Reed studied the case histories of 200 consecutive inpatients at Manchester Royal Infirmary who suffered from manic-depressive psychosis as defined by "classical" criteria. Their inpatients were no doubt more seriously ill than Brown's outpatients, though direct comparisons regarding specific symptoms or course of illness are impossible to make on the basis of information available in the two reports. Hopkinson and Reed did find their group to be similar to Brown's group with regard to sex distribution and mean age. Yet, when Hopkinson and Reed's inpatient depressives were compared to Brown's outpatient depressives, Brown's depressives had suffered a significantly higher frequency of loss of a father, loss of a mother, and loss of either parent. Hopkinson and Reed's manic-depressive psychotics were, on the other hand, found to be very similar to Brown's general population figures with respect to the frequency of each of these types of losses. Thus, the study by Hopkinson and Reed of manic-depressive psychotics, employing Brown's figures from the 1921 census as a control, is a negative study with regard to the association of childhood bereavement and adult depressive disorder. One is left wondering why patients who are apparently more ill than Brown's outpatients should be more like the normal controls with respect to the occurrence of childhood bereavement.

It should be noted that the difference regarding diagnostic formulation may not be the only difference between the two experimental groups. For example, no information is offered in either report regarding the social class of patients' parents. And, while Hopkinson and Reed's study of inpatient depressives appears to refute Brown's findings, a separate study (by Constance Dennehy, 1966), also comparing inpatient depressives with figures from the 1921 census, supports Brown's work.

The data for Dennehy's study were drawn from interviews with patients admitted to three hospitals in central London. Three hundred sixty-one of the patients interviewed were diagnosed by the consultant in charge of the case (some weeks after admission) as suffering depression (i.e., depression, reactive depression, agitated depression, involutional melancholia, or manic-depressive psychosis). When data from these 361 depressed patients were compared with the figures from the table on orphanhood of the 1921 census, both male and female depressives were found to suffer loss of a father before age 15 and loss of a mother before age 15 with significantly higher frequency than did "normals." (The differences between depressives and "normals" were significant for the age period 10 through 14, but not for earlier time periods.)

Dennehy's study answered two criticisms which have been leveled at the earlier works of Brown (1961) and Hopkinson and Reed (1966). First, data was based on interviews rather than "adequate" records. Second, it did investigate the influence of the ages of the subjects' parents (at the time of the subjects' birth) on its findings. Dennehy noted that the increased rate of childhood bereavement among the depressive patients were not confined to patients born to older parents; rather, the finding was consistent among all parental age groups. Yet, Dennehy's study may be criticized (as may Brown's) for comparing patients drawn from a hospital in a large urban area to members of the general population while failing to match the two groups for social class. Dennehy notes an excess of men from lower social classes in her patient sample. It is conceivable that such an excess may be responsible for the finding of an increased incidence of childhood bereavement in the depressive group.

Even if all criticisms of the studies were set aside, and the results from these three reports considered largely positive, they would not in themselves prove an association between childhood bereavement and depressive disorder, but only allow inferences regarding the association of childhood bereavement and psychiatric disorder in general. To prove a specific association of childhood bereavement with depressive disorder, comparisons of patients with depressive disorder versus patients with other psychiatric disorders would be necessary as well. We will review the evidence from just such comparisons in a later section. But first let us take a moment to review studies comparing depressive patients with medical patients (regarding incidence of childhood bereavement).

STUDIES COMPARING DEPRESSED PATIENTS WITH MEDICALLY ILL PATIENTS

The study by Felix Brown (1961), described in some detail in the previous section, included a control group of 267 medical-surgical inpatients and outpatients who were remarkably similar in average age to the 216 depressed outpatients under study. Brown found that only

19.6% of the medical-surgical controls had lost a parent (by death) before age 15, compared to 41% of his depressed patients. This 19.6% figure is very similar to the 16.6% frequency of childhood bereavement calculated for the general population from the 1921 census figures, and likewise is quite significantly less than the frequency in the depressed group, again confirming Brown's hypothesis of an association between childhood bereavement and depressive disorder.

Four other investigations comparing the frequency of childhood bereavement among depressed patients versus medically ill patients deserve mention. The first is a study by Forrest, Fraser, and Priest, reported in 1965. These authors acquired data regarding 48 depressed outpatients and 110 depressed inpatients plus (as controls) 58 patients under treatment in a general hospital for various medical and/or surgical conditions. They found that the depressed patients had suffered the loss of a parent before age 15 significantly more frequently than had the general hospital controls ($p < 0.05$). They reported that the depressed patients had lost a mother before age 15 more frequently than had controls (again, $p < 0.05$), but did not include in their report data regarding loss of a father.

In 1969, Munro and Griffiths reported information gathered from 10 psychiatrists regarding the inpatients and outpatients under their care for depressive disorder—a total of 162 patients. They compared the data regarding these patients with both of Brown's (1961) original control groups plus 100 "psychiatrically normal" general hospital outpatients whom they interviewed. While (as was the case in the study by Hopkinson and Reed, 1966) there were no differences regarding the frequency of a history of childhood bereavement between the depressive group and either of Brown's controls, there was a statistically significant ($p < 0.05$) excess of loss of a mother prior to age 15 among the inpatient, but not the outpatient, depressives when compared to general hospital controls.

While these two studies comparing depressed patients and medical-surgical patient controls offer some credence to the relationship between childhood parental loss (specifically, loss of a mother) and adult depressive disorder, at least two further studies of similar design failed to do so.

A study by Pitts *et al.* (1965) is perhaps the best designed study in this area to date. In that study, a structured interview was offered to consecutive admissions to St. Louis' Renard Hospital. A diagnosis of depressive disorder was made according to the criteria of Cassidy *et al.* (1957) and included clinical diagnoses of manic-depressive, psychotic depressive reaction, involutional psychotic reaction, and depressive reaction. Only patients with primary affective disorder (i.e., affective disorder pre-dating other diagnosable psychiatric disorders in any given individual) were included. The depressive group thus defined totaled 366 in number. Each diagnostic group (including the depressive group) was then characterized by age, sex, marital status, and socio-economic status. A stratified sample was constructed and controls were obtained from consecutive patients admitted to the obstetric, medical, and surgical services of Barnes Hospital who fit the appropriate cells of that sample. There were 180 controls in all. Finally, when the depressed patients were compared with the controls with regard to loss of a mother, loss of a father, or loss of either parent before age 15 (or during any of the three five-year periods contained therein), no significant differences were discovered.

One year later, Munro (1966) reported similar results from a similar study. Munro interviewed a group of depressed inpatients, again (as in the study by Pitts *et al.,* 1965) including only individuals with primary depressive disorder for study—153 in all. He then obtained 163 controls from a group of general hospital outpatients (excluding patients with a past history of affective disorder), whom he also interviewed. No differences were found between the depressives and controls with regard to age distribution, sex, social class distribution, or parental age at the time of the subjects' birth. Munro found that 21.6% of the depressives had lost a parent prior to age 16, compared to 20.2% of the medically ill controls. Thus, his study, like that of Pitts *et al.* (1965) was largely negative with regard to the association between childhood bereavement and adult depressive disorder. Munro did, however, note a tendency for a subgroup of patients with particularly severe depression to have experienced an excess of the death of a parent prior to the subjects' 16th birthday (a tendency which held true for loss of a mother, but not loss of a father). Munro in fact concluded that, while childhood deprivation is not important in the etiology of depressive disorder, it might well influence the severity of symptoms among depressive patients. This possibility will surface again later in our discussion.

Taken as a group, studies comparing depressed patients with medically ill patients fail to support the conclusions from comparisons between depressed patients and general population figures with regard to an association between childhood bereavement and depressive disorder. In particular, the more well-designed studies which included only primary depressives, including the one study which systematically obtained and matched experimental and control subjects, were negative in their findings.

Yet, it can be argued that the negative results of these studies are no more nor less than the result of their choice of medically ill patients as controls. After all, a significant number of patients who regularly attend general practitioners' practices are known to suffer psychiatric disturbances. Many suffer undiagnosed depressive disorder (although Munro (1966) and Munro and Griffiths (1969) did attempt to exclude such individuals). In any case, it can be argued that any large group of medically ill patients contains a significant number of individuals suffering other psychiatric illnesses which may themselves be associated with childhood bereavement and thus might obscure otherwise significant differences regarding the frequency of childhood bereavement among medically ill patients when compared to depressed patients. In the next section we will review those studies which compare the incidence of childhood bereavement among depressed patients versus patients with other psychiatric disorders.

STUDIES COMPARING DEPRESSED PATIENTS WITH PATIENTS WITH OTHER PSYCHIATRIC DISORDERS

In 1967, Hill and Price published a study of the records of first-admission psychiatric patients to the Maudsley Hospital, excluding patients with alcoholism and/or schizophrenia and patients with inadequate records, and otherwise including all of those patients with any depressive diagnosis in the case summary. In this fashion they accumulated an impressive total of 1,435 depressed patients. The remaining psychiatric patients (without a depressive diagnosis in the case summary) formed a control group of 1,007 patients in all. The authors discovered that 13.6% of the depressives had lost a father to death prior to their 15th birthday, compared to 8.9% of the controls

—a small but highly significant difference ($p < 0.001$). Differences regarding loss of a mother were negligible. The differences regarding father loss were noted to be consistent across decades of patient birth, more pronounced in females, and more pronounced with regard to loss between ages 10 to 14 (especially for females). The depressed patients were found, however, to have been born to older fathers than the controls, even after those who had been bereaved in childhood were excluded. This last finding suggests a primary association between parental age at subjects' birth (as opposed to childhood bereavement) and subsequent depressive disorder, though it does not explain the seemingly specific findings regarding the association of bereavement with females versus males and with later childhood versus earlier childhood. Interestingly, Hill and Price (1967) noted, in attempting to explain the importance of loss of a parent late in childhood, an earlier observation by Sylvia Anthony (1940) that a child's appreciation of death as a unique tragic event does not emerge until at least age 8; earlier loss may thus be assumed to result in more global disorders of personality, while later losses may presumably be associated with depressive disorder.

Two earlier studies by Beck's group deserve comment. In 1963, Beck, Sethi, and Tuthill reported the results of an interview study of 297 psychiatric inpatients and outpatients (excluding individuals with a diagnosis of brain damage). In addition to an interview, they administered each patient the Beck Depression Inventory (BDI) and simultaneously clinically rated each patient regarding the depth of his or her depression on a 4-point scale. They then divided the 297 patients into two groups, according to their scores on the BDI; those patients scoring 25 and above were considered "high depressed" (100 patients), while those scoring 13 or below were considered "non-depressed" (again, 100 patients).

Beck and associates found that 27% of the "high depressed" patients had lost a parent prior to age 16, compared to only 12% of the "non-depressed" patients ($p < 0.01$). A comparison between patients clinically rated as suffering "severe" depression versus those suffering "none" yielded very similar results. The difference was found to be consistent across all diagnostic categories; within each clinical diagnostic group, patients who scored highly on the BDI were more likely to have suffered the loss of a parent during childhood. Neither psychotic nor neurotic depressives, as a group, however, appeared to have suffered early parental loss more often than had patients in other diagnostic groups, contrary to the findings of Hill and Price (1967) noted earlier. This discrepancy may be the result of the relatively small number of patients studied by Beck, Sethi, and Tuthill, which would not allow the appreciation of small differences (such as the difference between 13.6% and 8.9% noted by Hill and Price).

A year after the first report from Beck's group, Sethi (1964) independently reported data derived in a very similar fashion. One hundred-sixteen psychiatric inpatients were studied. Again, each patient was administered the BDI and simultaneously clinically rated on a 4-point scale as regard to depth of his or her depression. Again, the patients were separated into "high depressed" versus "low depressed" subgroups, though the criteria employed by Sethi differed from those employed in the earlier investigation. Sethi defined "high depressed" patients as those (45 in all) with a clinical rating of moderate to severe depression plus a BDI score of 20 or more. The "low depressed" group (43 in number) were those with a clinical rating of no or low depression plus a BDI score of less than 20. Separating the two groups in this fashion, Sethi found no difference between "high" and "low" depressed patients regarding the frequency of childhood bereavement (i.e., death of a parent prior to age 16) in their histories; 15.5% of the "high depressed" patients had suffered such a loss compared to 16.3% of the "low depressed" patients.

One further study will be reviewed in this section. Birtchnell (1970) chose to study the records of 500 psychiatric admissions to Crichton Royal Hospital in Dumfries. Missing information was obtained by postal questionnaire and, if necessary, visits by mental welfare officers. The diagnosis of depression was made when depression appeared to be the "predominant" condition, and depressed patients were retrospectively rated regarding the depth of their depression on a 20-point scale (a score of 10 or more defined as severe). The depressed versus non-depressed, and severely versus moderately depressed, patient groups were then precisely matched for age.

When the depressed patients were subsequently compared to the non-depressed patients regarding the incidence of death of a parent prior to age 20, no differences were found (no differences regarding death of a parent, death of a mother, death of a father, or loss during any of the four five-year age spans prior to 20). However, when severely depressed patients were compared with moderately depressed patients, the severely depressed patients had experienced the loss of a mother prior to age 20 much more often than had the moderately depressed patients ($p < 0.001$).

To summarize, Hill and Price (1967), on the basis of samples of incredible size, found a small but significant association between the loss of a father during childhood and the development of depressive disorder (as opposed to other psychiatric disorders) as an adult. No subsequent study has succeeded in replicating those results. The studies by Beck's group (Beck, Sethi, and Tuthill, 1963; Sethi, 1964) drew comparisons among psychiatric patients on the basis of scores on the Beck Depression Inventory, rather than on the basis of clinical diagnoses, and obtained equivocal results. Birtchnell's study (1970) found no differences between psychiatric patients with and without a clinical diagnosis of depression as regards childhood parental loss, though loss of a mother during childhood was noted more often among the patients with severe depressions than among those with moderate depressions (precisely the finding of Munro, 1966). Thus, all in all, these studies failed to support any distinction of depressive patients (as opposed to patients with other psychiatric disorders) as particularly likely to have suffered the loss of a parent during childhood.

The reader must be reminded however, that these studies do suffer serious methodological defects which could conceivably minimize otherwise important differences between depressed patients and other psychiatric patients. None of the studies cited clearly separated patients with primary depressive disorder from those with secondary depressive disorder. The depressed groups thus may be contaminated by patients suffering any of a number of other psychiatric illnesses whose degree of association with childhood bereavement is yet undetermined. It is conceivable that a more homogeneously primary depressive population might be found to differ more markedly from patients with other psychiatric disorders regarding their frequency of childhood bereavement than have the heterogeneous groups studied to date.

Further, it should be noted that any studies employing patients (either medically ill patients or psychiatrically ill patients) as controls are subject to criticism for their choice of control group. Experts have argued that the loss of a parent during childhood may predispose an individual toward dependent behaviors during adulthood, including the seeking of medical help more readily than other individuals. All patients thus may share an increased frequency of childhood bereavement compared to non-patients which blurs the differences between various patient groups. This particular criticism is answered in the final study to be reviewed in this chapter.

THE WORK OF GEORGE W. BROWN

George W. Brown and his colleagues have in the past several years published a number of reports based upon an important and intriguing study of the women living in Camberwell, a suburb of London. Their study will be discussed in considerable detail in the next chapter. Because a portion of their work is pertinent to the current discussion of the association between depressive disorder and childhood bereavement, their investigation and relevant findings will be briefly presented in the paragraphs that follow (based upon Brown, Harris, and Copeland, 1977).

Brown and his associates interviewed 114 women living in Camberwell and undergoing treatment (either inpatient or outpatient) for the diagnosis of primary depressive illness. They then randomly sampled the remaining women in Camberwell and administered each woman in that sample a modified version of the Present State Exam (PSE), in order to determine the presence or absence of a number of psychiatric symptoms in the subjects. On the basis of the results of the PSE, 76 women were identified as suffering a definite psychiatric disorder the year prior to interview. All of these women were suffering from recognized clinical syndromes, almost exclusively affective in nature. These women Brown and his colleagues labeled "cases," i.e., women with depressive disorder not in current treatment. The remainder of the random sample of women in the community, 382 women in all, did not show evidence of definite psychiatric disorder on the basis of the PSE and were used as normal controls.

When Brown, Harris, and Copeland (1977) then compared the "cases" with "normals," they found a significantly higher frequency of loss of a mother before age 11 among the "cases" ($p < 0.01$). Yet, in comparing the group of depressed patients with the women in the general population (either including or excluding the identified "cases" of depressive disorder), no significant differences were discovered.

On the basis of these findings, Brown suggests that childhood bereavement, particularly loss of a mother prior to age 11, serves as a vulnerability factor, predisposing women to the subsequent occurrence of depressive disorder in adulthood. This conclusion must clearly be based on the evidence from his comparison of "cases" with "normals," rather than depressed patients with "normals." But Brown has an explanation for his failure to find evidence for his conclusion in the comparison of depressed patients and his non-patient group. His reasoning is essentially as follows: among the subjects of his study, the loss of a mother before age 11 was strongly associated with the presence of 3 or more children under age 14 in the subject's home at the time of interview; the presence of 3 or more children under age 14 in the subject's home was strongly associated with a decreased likelihood that the subject would contact a physician when depressed; thus, the loss of a mother before age 11 was correlated with a decreased likelihood of contacting a physician, i.e., a decreased likelihood of "patienthood." The argument is interesting, but clearly contradicts the assumption of other authors (noted earlier) that childhood bereavement is likely to predispose an individual towards dependent behaviors, including the seeking of patienthood, as an adult. Further, one wonders whether the series of statistical correlations upon which Brown's argument is based (specifically, the association of loss of a mother and subsequent fertility) would be found in other populations.

As a final note, the 114 patients studied by Brown and his colleagues were rated as either psychotic or neurotic on the basis of available clinical material, and further rated (independently of the distinction as psychotic or neurotic) as to the severity of their symptoms on admission to treatment. Brown, Harris, and Copeland (1977) found that 77% of the more psychotic group of patients, compared to 42% of the lesser psychotic patients, and only 16% of the neurotic group of patients had suffered a past loss (of a parent or sibling) through death ($p < 0.01$). This evidence points (as did the earlier work of Munro, 1966, and Birtchnell, 1970) to a relationship between early loss and the formation of symptoms of depression in adult life. Specifically, once again, early loss was associated with more severe symptomatology among those who develop depressive disorder in adulthood. It should be noted, however, that (in contrast to earlier studies) Brown and his colleagues included losses of siblings as well as parents, and did not strictly confine these losses to the period of childhood.

DISCUSSION

The studies summarized in this chapter provide unconvincing, often contradictory, evidence as to the association of depressive disorder and childhood bereavement. Certainly, it could be argued that such an association exists in reality, and that the inconsistent results of research have been due to any of a number of methodological problems which continue to plague the area. No doubt, additional studies of sound methodological design (e.g., involving individual interviews rather than chart reviews, employing a criteria-based definition of depressive disorder such as that offered by DSM–III, restricting study to patients with primary depressive disorder, and matching those individuals with control groups with regard to geographical location, age of subjects, age of subjects' parents at the time of subjects' birth, and social class of the subjects' parents) are still indicated. And more than one study will be required. Studies comparing depressed patients (or non-patients for that matter) with general population controls may suggest an association between childhood bereavement and depressive disorder. It cannot prove such an association to be specific to depressive disorder, however, without either additional studies comparing individuals with depressive disorder versus individuals with other psychiatric disorders or, on the other hand, studies comparing individuals with other psychiatric disorders with general population controls. Without such additional studies, only an association between childhood bereavement and psychiatric illness is implied.

One must wonder, in muddling through all of this, whether there are not more basic problems in such an approach than simply the methodological nightmares already noted. Perhaps the very concepts employed to date are overly simplistic. Intuitively, more than the mere fact of a loss of a parent must be considered in determining the influence of that impact on a child's subsequent development, factors such as the relationship between the child and that parent prior to the parent's death, the age (and emotional maturity) of the child at the time of the parent's death, and the child's environment subsequent to the loss. Perhaps it is not simply the loss of the parent, but rather the loss of a loved parent, or the loss of a parent in the absence of an available parent substitute, that predispose a child to the subsequent development of depression.

Moreover, even if certain parental losses do serve as a vulnerability factor, predisposing an individual to the development of depressive disorder as an adult, the influence of such losses may become apparent only in the presence of other, precipitating, events in later life. In the next chapter we will explore the literature in search of the evidence for the existence of such precipitants of depressive disorder in adult life.

REFERENCES

Abraham, K.: A short study of the development of the libido, viewed in the light of mental disorders. In *Selected Papers on Psychoanalysis,* pp. 418–501. Hogarth Press, London, 1942.

Anthony, S.: *The Child's Discovery of Death.* Kegan Paul, London, 1940.

Beck, A.T., Sethi, B.B., and Tuthill, R.W.: Childhood bereavement and adult depression. *Arch. Gen. Psychiat., 9*:295–302, 1963.

Birtchnell, J.: Depression in relation to early and recent parent death. *Brit. J. Psychiat., 116*:299–306, 1970.

Brown, F.: Depression and childhood bereavement. *J. Ment. Sci., 107*:754–777, 1961.

Brown, G.W., Harris, T., and Copeland, J.R.: Depression and loss. *Brit. J. Psychiat., 130*:1–18, 1977.

Cassidy, W.L., Flanagan, N.B., Spellman, M., and Cohen, M.E.: Clinical observations in manic-depressive disease. *J.A.M.A., 164*:1535–1546, 1957.

Dennehy, C.M.: Childhood bereavement and psychiatric illness. *Brit. J. Psychiat. 112*:1049–1069, 1966.

Forrest, A.D., Fraser, R.H., and Priest, R.G.: Environmental factors in depressive illness. *Brit. J. Psychiat., 111*:243–253, 1965.

Gregory, I: Studies of parental deprivation in psychiatric patients. *Am. J. Psychiat., 115*:432–442, 1958.

Hill, O.W., and Price, J.S.: Childhood bereavement and adult depression. *Brit. J. Psychiat., 113*:743–751, 1967.

Hopkinson, G., and Reed, G.F.: Bereavement in childhood and depressive psychosis. *Brit. J. Psychiat., 112*:459–463, 1966.

Munro, A.: Parental deprivation in depressive patients. *Brit. J. Psychiat., 112*:443–457, 1966.

Munro, A., and Griffiths, A.B.: Some psychiatric non-sequelae of childhood bereavement. *Brit. J. Psychiat., 115*:305–311, 1969.

Pitts, F.N., Jr., Meyer, J., Brooks, M., and Winokur, G.: Adult psychiatric illness assessed for childhood parental loss, and psychiatric illness in family members—a study of 748 patients and 250 controls. *Am. J. Psychiat., 121*:i–x, 1965.

Sethi, B.B.: Relationship of separation to depression. *Arch. Gen. Psychiat., 10*:486–496, 1964.

SUGGESTED FURTHER READING

Lloyd, C.: Life events and depressive disorder reviewed—I. Events as predisposing factors. *Arch. Gen. Psychiat., 37*:529–535, 1980.

Tennant, C., Bebbington, P., and Hurry, J.: Parental death in childhood and risk of adult depressive disorders: a review. *Psychol. Med., 10*:289–299, 1980.

Tennant, C., Hurry, J., and Bebbington, P.: The relation of childhood separation experiences to adult depressive and anxiety states. *Brit. J. Psychiat., 141*:475–482, 1982.

Chapter 5

LIFE EVENTS AND DEPRESSIVE DISORDER

Everyday events at times produce alterations in one's emotions. Realization of a loss, whether it be of one's wallet, pet, or relative, may well result in one's feeling sad. And there exists an obvious relationship between sadness and depressive disorder. Sadness is, after all, frequently the most obvious symptom of depressive disorder. And there are those who view depressive disorder as simply an extreme form of sadness. If one accepts this view, one might readily assume then that extreme life events (for example, profound losses) might precipitate, and even be entirely responsible for, episodes of depressive disorder. In psychiatry today, while it is accepted that certain catastrophic events (e.g., exposure to combat, concentration camps, or natural disasters) may produce both physical and psychological casualties, there remains considerable debate as to whether less extraordinary events bear a causal relationship to diagnosable psychiatric disorder, especially affective illness.

Earlier in the century, psychoanalysts theorized that all depressions are precipitated by the loss of a loved object, either an actual or a fantasied loss. If the loss responsible for the depression was not apparent, it then behooved the therapist to seek in the patient's unconscious the roots of his illness. Others, more empirically inclined, rejected certain precepts of psychoanalytic theory and chose to dichotomize patients' depressive episodes into those apparently precipitated by an actual environmental event (i.e., exogenous depressions) and, on the other hand, those with no apparent relationship to life circumstances (i.e., endogenous depressions). In recent decades, many have attempted to separate exogenous (or reactive) from endogenous depressions according to differences in symptomatology (as noted in Chapter 2). Unfortunately, evidence of a consistent relationship between such exogenous or endogenous symptom complexes and the presence or absence, respectively, of some precipitating life event has not been forthcoming. Efforts to clearly define a subgroup of depressive disorders precipitated (or caused) by life events have thus been unsuccessful. Indeed, with the development of somatic therapies (i.e., electroconvulsive therapy and the antidepressants) effective in the treatment of depressive disorder and the accumulation of evidence in favor of genetic influences in its etiology, the burden of proof has shifted to those who maintain that life events are causally related to any substantial subgroup of affective disorders.

One related issue is in need of immediate clarification. One life event, one very real loss, that is, the death of a spouse, is commonly associated with the appearance of a depressive syndrome in the surviving partner. Clayton (1979), in a review of her prospective study of 109 widows and widowers, noted that 45% of these subjects met the Feighner criteria (see Chapter 2) for depression at some point during the year after their loss. In other words, nearly half of those individuals who lose a spouse will manifest a condition identical in appearance to Major Depression soon after their loss.

In modern society, though, this condition (Uncomplicated Bereavement, according to DSM–III), this dramatic alteration in affect, is seen as a normal response to the loss of a spouse, not as a disease. Bereaved individuals rarely seek medical or psychiatric assistance during the course of their bereavement. And psychiatrists rarely treat bereaved individuals as they would individuals presenting with depressive disorder without a recent history of bereavement. The American Psychiatric Association in the Third Edition of its *Diagnostic and Statistical Manual* (1980) classifies Uncomplicated Bereavement among conditions not attributable to a mental disorder. (If, in the clinician's judgment, a patient's bereavement is unduly severe or prolonged, the clinician may change the diagnosis from Uncomplicated Bereavement to Major Depression. While such is not often the case, 13% of the widows and widowers studied by Clayton (1979) met criteria for depressive disorder for the entire year after their loss.)

Given that the death of a spouse is often associated with a depressive syndrome, but not with depressive disorder as defined by our society, what of the association of other life events and affective illness?

If catastrophic events can be linked causally with depressive illness, can one reject entirely the significance of other less dramatic life events?

In Chapter 4, it was noted that certain methodological difficulties were inherent in investigations of the association between childhood bereavement and depressive disorder. Unfortunately, the same is true of investigations of the association between life events and depressive disorder. At least four issues regarding the design of any study of the association of life events and depressive disorder need to be kept in mind in reviewing this literature.

The first essential step in studying the relationship between life events and depressive disorder is the selection of a uniform clinical group, i.e., a clearly defined sample of depressed patients for investigation. In other words, the investigator must begin with a clear definition of depressive disorder. Historical problems in this regard were noted in the last chapter. Difficulties due to the varying definitions of depressive disorder which permeated the studies reviewed in Chapter 4 similarly compromise our ability to make definitive conclusions regarding the literature to be reviewed in this chapter.

Assuming that an investigation includes an acceptable, criteria-based definition of depressive disorder, the second methodological hurdle lies in the selection of specific life events for study. You will no doubt recollect from the previous chapter that most individuals researching the relationship between childhood deprivation and adult depressive disorder settled on studying childhood bereavement as a reasonably objectifiable and quantifiable childhood event. Unfortunately, few other life events are as objectifiable or quantifiable. Individuals interested in researching the relationship between life events (other than bereavement) and adult depressive disorder must decide which life events are relevant to study. Investigators have often developed idiosyncratic research designs in this respect.

Holmes and Rahe (1967) developed the Social Readjustment Rating Scale for use in studies of the association of life events and any of a number of physical and psychological conditions. They composed a list of 43 life events empirically derived from clinical experience as, in their opinions, relevant to the subsequent development of physical and psychological disorders. They then asked a sample of convenience of 394 subjects to rate each of the 43 events as to the relative degree of necessary social readjustment (the amount and duration of change in life pattern, regardless of its desirability) entailed by each event for the average person. The authors set an arbitrary rating of 500 for the social readjustment necessitated by the event of marriage, and asked their subjects to rate the other 42 events accordingly. They thus obtained weighted values for the social readjustment required by each of the 43 life events on their list. Assuming that social readjustments required by different events are cumulative within a specified period of time, their scale then offers an estimate (calibrated in Life Change Units) of the overall adjustment demanded by the life events experienced by any given individual in a given period of time. The Social Readjustment Rating Scale (SRRS) has subsequently been used by a large number of investigators studying relationships between life events and a large number of somatic and psychological disorders.

Once depressive disorder is defined and life events selected for study, the investigator must identify some means of accurately identifying and dating the occurrence of those events in the lives of the experimental subjects. Obviously, it is of particular importance for the investigator to be able to date the life events in question relative to the onset of depressive disorder in each individual subject. Again we are faced with the problems posed by the retrospective nature of all of the studies in this area to date. Studies regarding the relationship between life events and depressive disorder have invariably begun with the identification of a group of depressed individuals whose histories are then combed for the occurrence of any of a number of life events in the weeks or months prior to the onset of their depressive episodes. Given this retrospective approach, the inaccuracies entailed by limiting the review of the patients' histories (for life events) to a review of hospital records are obvious. Even if, in addition, subjects are individually interviewed at length regarding the occurrence of particular life events in their recent past, methodological difficulties persist. Everyone has difficulty recalling the occurrence of specific life events which took place more than a few months ago. Even if a subject were able to recall essential life events, he or she might well not be disposed to revealing information of such a personal nature to a stranger during a single interview. (An ongoing relationship, usually with a therapist, may be necessary to elicit details regarding the occurrence of life events prior to the onset of a depressive episode).

Further, the occurrence of any particular event and/or the importance of that event may be exaggerated by an individual during a depressive episode. The significance of events occurring early during the insidious development of a depressive episode, a time during which an individual may be particularly easily upset by even trivial events, may well be magnified by the patient's illness. In addition, depressive illness may itself produce new events which likely would not otherwise have occurred. Any given event may be the result, rather than the cause, of a depressive episode. In fact, Hudgens (1974) pointed out that 29 of the 43 items included in the Social Readjustment Rating Scale of Holmes and Rahe are often symptoms or consequences of depressive illness. For example, event #38 on the SRRS—change in sleeping habits—is frequently a symptom of depressive disorder, while event #19—change in arguments with one's spouse—is often a consequence of depressive disorder. For this reason, the investigator is obliged to attempt to date specific life events relative to the onset of depressive disorder, and to restrict his or her consideration to those events indisputably dated prior to the onset to depressive symptoms. Even if the investigator succeeds in this rather difficult task, the critic may argue that depressed individuals often scan their previous lives in search of events to explain their current guilt and gloom, events which might give meaning to their illness; depressed individuals might well then report more life events in a given period of their histories than would normals. For this reason, it may be argued that the subject should be interviewed regarding life events only after their depressive symptoms have abated in order to minimize any confounding effect due to their depressed mental state (even though this increases the period of time between the event and the expectation that the individual will recall the event, thus increasing the likelihood that forgetfulness will confound the results).

In an effort to minimize these problems, information may be enlisted from additional informants such as family members. Hudgens, Robins, and Delong (1970), however, found a discouragingly low rate of agreement between 80 recently admitted psychiatric patients and 103 of their relatives, all of whom were given a structured interview regarding the life stresses suffered by the patients during the year prior to admission. There was only 57% overall agreement between patients and their relatives as to whether specific stresses had occurred during that year, and only 26% agreement as to whether specific stresses were causally related to the onset of illness. Those authors concluded that their results cast doubt on the validity of any retrospective studies in this area.

Assuming an investigator is able satisfactorily to define depressive disorder, select life events for study, and identify those events relative to the onset of depressive disorder in the experimental subjects, there remains the final major methodological problem of specifying a control group. Briefly, the control subjects should resemble the experimental (i.e., depressed) subjects in as many respects as possible, with the possible exception that their histories should be free of psychiatric illness, specifically affective disorder. Yet, a growing body of evidence suggests that life events may be associated with the onset of a vast array of somatic and psychological disorders, and perhaps patienthood itself. Thus, it may be argued that the failure to find differences regarding the frequency of life events predating depressive disorder as compared to other psychiatric or medical disorders may be due to the simple fact that given life events are causally related to both depressive disorder and any other psychiatric or medical disorder under study. On the other hand, it may be argued that differences regarding the frequency of life events in the histories of depressed patients as compared to "normals" are related simply to the fact that the experimental group consists of patients, implying a relationship between life events and patienthood rather than a specific relationship between life events and depressive disorder.

You may have already noted that I have not, as I did in Chapter 4, made any attempt to dissuade the reader from wading through the literature review to follow. This is not to imply that the following review will be any less confusing or any more likely to lend itself to definitive conclusions than does the literature regarding childhood bereavement and depressive disorder. No doubt my desire to have you accompany me in the journey through the literature regarding life events and depressive disorder is in part a matter of personal preference; I simply find the subject matter much more stimulating—and I am not alone in this regard. While active investigation of the association between childhood bereavement and adult depressive disorder virtually ceased 10 years ago (except for the inclusion of childhood bereavement as one of several vulnerability factors in the work of

George W. Brown and his colleagues), research regarding the association of life events and depressive disorder is not only alive and well but thriving and veritably exploding in the past few years. Thus, familiarity with the issues involved and attempts to derive conclusions from the information gathered to date (and to direct future research), are much more relevant.

EARLY STUDIES EMPLOYING MEDICALLY ILL CONTROL GROUPS

Forrest, Fraser and Priest (1965), in an investigation cited in the last chapter, studied 158 depressed patients and 58 general hospital inpatients (as controls). They obtained on each patient a schedule of data which included a variety of social and medical factors occurring during the three years prior to their admission to hospital (or referral to outpatient care). They found no significant difference between the two groups (depressed patients versus medically ill patients) with regard to the frequency with which patients had experienced bereavement or medical problems during that period of time. They did note, however, that social factors, specifically isolation and loss of social role, were reported more frequently by patients in the depressed group ($p < 0.01$). While these results might be interpreted as implying that social factors are important in the etiology of depressive disorder, it should be noted that the authors made no attempt to date the events under study relative to the onset of depression. The authors themselves noted that these factors, i.e., isolation and loss of social role, may simply be symptoms of the illness itself rather than causal factors. Thus, the inadequate design of the study makes conclusions regarding a causal relationship between life events and depressive disorder impossible.

In 1967, Hudgens, Morrison, and Barchha reported the results of their study of 40 patients hospitalized with a diagnosis with primary affective disorder (34 depressed and 6 manic), whose onset of illness could be dated with considerable precision. As a control group, they selected 40 patients admitted to non-psychiatric services who had no history of psychiatric symptoms sufficient to result in impairment or hospitalization. The mood-disordered patients and the medically ill patients were matched regarding sex, marital status, age and race. And no difference was found between the two groups regarding social class distribution. Both patients and controls were administered a standardized interview which included a systematic inquiry into the occurrence of a large number of life events. Events were recorded as having occurred if they were considered "important" by the patient (whether or not the investigator agreed) or the investigator (whether or not the patient agreed). A patient's relative was also interviewed in similar fashion when available and when any question regarding a patient's reliability existed.

Ten of the 40 patients hospitalized for affective disorder reported the occurrence of one or more definitely stressful event preceding the first sign of the current episode of illness. The authors noted, however, that 8 of these 10 patients had experienced other very important events earlier in their lives without the development of affective disorder (in the ensuing year). Overall, no significant differences were discovered between the mood-disordered patients and the medically ill patients regarding the frequency of remote or recent losses, history of remote or recent hospitalization for medical or surgical reasons, or job changes during the year prior to admission. Indeed, the only significant differences between the two groups were that the affective patients more frequently reported discord at home or at work in the year prior to admission and a change of dwelling in the year prior to admission. The authors noted that both differences could be explained as results, rather than causes, of illness (in fact, of the 14 affectively disordered patients who had changed dwellings in the year prior to admission, only five did so prior to the onset of their illness).

Thus, both of these early studies comparing depressed patients with medically ill patients found little evidence for a specific association between depressive disorder and life events. As noted earlier, though, it is entirely conceivable that certain life events, or an accumulation of various life events, may predispose both toward depressive disorder and to any of a variety of medical illnesses. For this reason, studies comparing depressed patients with physically (and psychiatrically) "well" controls are of value. Such a comparison was undertaken in the next investigation to be reviewed.

THE NEW HAVEN STUDY

In 1969, Paykel and associates reported the results of their study performed in New Haven, Connecticut. They chose for study in that community 185 patients (a mixture of inpatients and outpatients) suffering depression defined as follows: a disorder in which the central feature is depressed affect (which might be accompanied by guilt, worthlessness, hopelessness, and/or suicidal feelings), at least one week in duration, and rated 2 or more on a global severity-of-illness scale (calibrated from 0–6), excluding patients in which depressed mood is secondary to other predominant symptomatology. It should be noted at this point that Paykel and his associates thus selected for study a group of patients with rather mild depressive symptoms; it might even be questioned whether their diagnostic criteria would clearly demarcate depressive disorder from more common, situational moodswings. This is perhaps the most profound defect of the study.

One hundred eighty-five control subjects were selected from an epidemiologic survey of the same community, i.e., New Haven. Each control subject was matched to a depressed patient along parameters of sex, age, marital status, race, and social class. Both depressed patients and control subjects were given a semi-structured interview which included inquiry as to the occurrence of 33 events (modified from the Social Readjustment Rating Scale) during the six months prior to onset of illness (for depressed patients) or interview (for controls). Depressed patients were interviewed only after their depressive symptoms were much improved, to diminish any distortion in recall due to their mood disorder.

Overall, the depressed patients reported nearly three times as many life events as did controls (an average of 1.69 events per depressed patient compared to 0.59 events per control subject during the six months in question). Of the 33 events studied, 8 events were reported significantly more often (at the 5% level) by the depressed patients: increase in arguments with spouse, marital separation, start of new type of work, death of immediate family member, serious illness of family member, departure of family member from home, serious personal physical illness, and change in work condition.

With these results in mind, the authors re-examined their list of life events and grouped events into categories in three ways. First, they categorized events as to whether they involved a departure (exit) of an individual from a subject's social field, or, on the other hand, the entrance of a new person into a subject's social field. Exit events were found to have occurred in 46 of the depressed patients, compared to only 9 of the controls ($p < 0.01$), while entrances were equally distributed between the two groups. Next, the authors divided the list of life events into those which they considered clearly desirable versus those which seemed clearly undesirable. Undesirable events were reported much more frequently ($p < 0.01$) by depressed patients (82 patients) than controls (31 subjects), while desirable events were reported considerably less often by both groups and with approximately the same frequency by both groups. Finally, the authors categorized events into the areas of social activity which they involved. Depressives reported more events than controls in all areas of activity; this third categorization did not discriminate between groups in the same manner as did the first two categorizations.

The authors (Paykel *et al.,* 1969) concluded that the "most plausible explanation" of their findings is a causative relationship between the life events reported in excess by depressed patients (specifically, exits from the social field and undesirable events) and depressive disorder. They noted that a simple life-change model attempting to relate the onset of depressive disorder to the magnitude of change in life pattern necessitated by life events—irrespective of desirability—is likely insufficient; rather, different events would appear to have different implications for the individual and different potential regarding the precipitation of a depressive episode. Specifically, exits from the social field and socially undesirable events appeared much more potent in this regard than did other events in the New Haven study.

Though Paykel *et al.* (1969) voiced their dissatisfaction with the life-change model (and presumably, the use of the SRRS in studies of life events and depressive disorder), Paykel, Prusoff, and Uhlenhuth (1971) subsequently undertook a series of studies replicating and extending the earlier work of Holmes and Rahe in scaling life events. They developed their own list of life events containing a total of 61 events (derived from the SRRS) and asked a group of 373 subjects (213 psychiatric patients and 160 relatives of patients) to evaluate the events as to how upsetting the event would be to the average person, using a 0–20 scale with no event being fixed in value. The authors thus derived a scale of life events, ranked according to the mean score given each event by the group of 373 subjects from most upsetting (death of child, mean score of 19.33) to least upsetting (child married with respondent's approval, mean score of 2.94). This scale could then be used in subsequent research regarding the relationship of depressive disorder and life events.

In 1974, with this new life event scale in hand, Paykel returned to the initial data from the New Haven study. Clinically, few of the 185 depressed patients in the original New Haven experimental group seemed to be suffering endogenous depression; only about 15% of the cases appeared to have been unprecipitated by one or more life events. With factor analysis techniques, however, it was possible in reviewing the data regarding depressed patients' symptoms to identify a bipolar factor contrasting endogenous versus neurotic (or reactive) symptom clusters. And it was possible, with the method of scaling life events described above, to allot to each depressed patient a "score" by summing the scaled scores for each of the life events which had been reported as occurring in the six months prior to the onset of his or her depressive episode. Paykel (1974) found the correlation between the endogenous/neurotic symptom factor and patients' stress scores to be so weak as to be trivial. In other words, Paykel found no evidence for an association between stressful life events and either neurotic or endogenous depressive disorder.

EARLIER STUDIES COMPARING SUBTYPES OF DEPRESSIVE DISORDER

This is probably as good a point as any to digress for a moment and review a question related to whether or not depressive disorder is related to life events—i.e., whether any one subtype of depressive disorder is more strongly related to life events than any other. As noted earlier, depressive illness was historically divided into exogenous versus endogenous subtypes, according to whether or not the disorder was deemed clinically to have been precipitated by some life event. As also noted, the reactive (or neurotic) and endogenous subtypes were each subsequently defined by certain symptom complexes. Intuitively, it would seem likely that the reactive (or neurotic) depressive syndrome would be shown to be more strongly associated with precipitating life events than the endogenous depressive syndrome. Further, in view of the evidence presented in Chapter 3 to the effect that a stronger case exits for a genetic (i.e., biological) basis for bipolar than unipolar depressive disorder, it might be assumed that a stronger relationship to environmental causation (i.e., life events) could be shown for a unipolar than bipolar depressive disorder. Paykel (1974), however, was unable to demonstrate a stronger association between neurotic depressive symptomatology and life events than between endogenous symptomatology and life events. At least three other studies worth noting likewise failed to distinguish between endogenous and neurotic depressive subtypes as regards their association with life events.

Forrest, Fraser, and Priest (1965), in a study cited earlier in this chapter, provided data regarding 158 depressed patients. Of these 158 patients, the authors dichotomized 105 into either endogenous (62 patients) or neurotic (43 patients) subgroups on the basis of whether or not they exhibited at least 4 of 5 endogenous symptoms. The investigators gathered information from each patient with regard to a variety of social and medical factors occurring during the three years prior to their admission to hospital or referral to outpatient care. The authors found no difference between the endogenous and neurotic groups regarding the occurrence of either social or medical factors during the time period under study.

In 1970, Leff, Roatch, and Bunney reported the findings from their study of 40 consecutive admissions to a research ward at the National Institute of Mental Health. Criteria for admission to that ward included feelings of hopelessness and worthlessness, thoughts of death and suicide, and severely depressed mood. 13 of the 40 patients demonstrated at least 5 of 6 endogenous characteristics and were defined as endogenously depressed; the remaining 27 patients were defined as non-endogenous. All "stressful" environmental events occurring within one year prior to the point of "breakdown in functioning" were dated and analyzed. The authors discovered no difference between the endogenous and non-endogenous groups regarding either the overall incidence or specific types of stressful environmental events in the period under study.

Finally, I will mention a report by Thomson and Hendrie in 1972 which is consistent with the previously cited studies. Thomson and Hendrie interviewed 74 consecutive inpatients diagnosed as suffering primary depressive illness (excluding patients with illness secondary to alcoholism, drug abuse, or schizophrenia). Ten of the 74 patients were interviewed on admission, the remaining patients interviewed just prior to discharge (presumably after their depressive symptoms had abated). For each patient, the interview included administration of the Social Readjustment Rating Scale for the year prior to the onset of the index depressive episode. Two control groups were selected for study, the first a group of 37 members and friends of the hospital staff, the second a group of 22 patients suffering early polyarthritis. Each control subject was administered the SRRS for the year prior to interview. The depressed group was found to have a significantly higher mean life-change score than either control group. Unfortunately, though both control groups were matched to the depressed group with regard to age and sex, they were not matched along lines of social class, and indeed lower social classes were overrepresented in the depressed group, tempering any conclusions which might otherwise be derived from the study. Within the depressed group, patients were clinically separated into endogenous versus reactive-neurotic subgroups; no significant difference was found between these two depressive subtypes with regard to mean life-change scores.

Certainly, each of the above studies may be faulted for its own individual methodological inadequacies, but on the basis of the evidence available from this group of studies taken as a whole, no clear evidence exists that either the neurotic or the endogenous subtype is more or less associated with precipitating life events than the other.

Two other studies have attempted to determine whether unipolar depressive disorder is more often precipitated by some life event than is bipolar affective disorder. In 1973, Clancy and associates published data based on a review of the records of all patients consecutively admitted to the Iowa Psychiatric Hospital beginning in 1935. Patients were included for study if, according to their records, they met Feighner criteria for primary affective disorder. Altogether, 225 unipolar patients and 100 bipolar patients were included. Their records were scanned for events which might have precipitated the onset of their illness; events were recorded as precipitants if judged to be severely stressful and to have occurred during the three months prior to the onset of affective disturbance. 39% of the unipolar patients were deemed to have experienced a precipitating event, compared to only 27% of the bipolar patients ($p < 0.05$).

A similar study by Perris (1966), however, reports conflicting results. Perris interviewed 150 patients with recurrent psychotic depression and 145 patients with bipolar affective disorder, noting any and all somatic and psychological precipitating factors occurring in the three months before the onset of the current episode of illness. 39% of the unipolar patients and 34% of the bipolar patients reported at least one such precipitating event—a nonsignificant difference.

Thus, the available research evidence regarding the association of life events with the onset of unipolar as compared to bipolar affective disorder is contradictory. The Perris study (1966), which is methodologically the sounder of the two studies in that it employs patient interviews rather than chart reviews, is negative in its findings. (For a recent study and review of the literature regarding the association between life events and manic episodes in bipolar patients, as compared to non-depressive control groups, see Kennedy *et al.,* 1983.)

To date, research evidence fails to support popularly held opinions regarding a preferential association between life events and any subtype of depressive disorder (i.e., either exogenous or unipolar subtypes).

STUDIES COMPARING DEPRESSIVE DISORDER WITH SCHIZOPHRENIA

As noted in the previous section, Clancy *et al.* (1973) reviewed the records of consecutive admissions to the Iowa Psychiatric Hospital beginning in 1935. In this way, they collected records regarding 225 patients with unipolar depressive disorder, 100 patients with bipolar affective illness, and 200 patients suffering schizophrenia (according to Feighner criteria). They combed the records for life events and recorded an event as having precipitated the index episode of illness if the event was judged by the investigators to have been severely stressful and to have occurred within three months prior to onset. While 39% of the unipolar patients and 27% of the bipolar patients were reported to have experienced an event which precipitated their illness, only 11% of the schizophrenics related a similar event. The difference between bipolar patients and schizophrenic patients in this regard was highly significant ($p < 0.01$). As previously suggested, the study by Clancy *et al.* was less than ideal in research design, particularly in its use of a chart review methodology, and required replication.

Jacobs, Prusoff, and Paykel (1974) gathered 50 first-admission patients satisfying research criteria for schizophrenia and matched with them, as completely as possible, 50 of the 185 depressed patients derived from the earlier study by Paykel *et al.* (1969)—with regard to age, sex, marital status, race, and social class. As the interview of depressed patients had been delayed until symptoms had subsided, so the interview of schizophrenics was likewise delayed for at least two weeks after admission to allow acute symptoms to abate. The interview included a list of 59 events covering a wide range of occurrences and covered the 6 months immediately prior to onset for both groups.

Depressed patients reported more events than did schizophrenic patients (an average of 3.6 events per depressed patient, compared to 2.5 events per schizophrenic patient; $p < 0.05$), more undesirable events (44 depressed patients reporting at least one such event, compared to 34 schizophrenic patients; $p < 0.05$), more exits from the social field (23 depressed patients reporting at least one such event, compared to 12 schizophrenic patients; $p < 0.05$), and more interpersonal arguments (26 depressed patients reporting at least one such event, compared to 9 schizophrenic patients; $p < 0.001$). There was no difference between the depressed and the schizophrenic groups with regard to the frequency with which desirable events or entrances to the social field were reported. This data thus supported the findings of the earlier study by Paykel *et al.* (1969) in suggesting that exits from the social field and undesirable events are specifically related to the subsequent occurrence of depressive disorder (as opposed to schizophrenia or no disorder at all).

In a subsequent review of his own research, Paykel (1979) points out that exits from the social field, undesirable events and interpersonal arguments all occur with a higher frequency during the six months prior to the onset of both depressive disorder and schizophrenia than they do in a given 6-month period in members of the general population. Thus, these 3 categories of events are statistically associated with the onset of both depressive disorder and schizophrenia, though the relationship for all three categories is much stronger with depressive disorder than with schizophrenia. Paykel further asserts that the exit/entrance distinction, the exit: entrance ratio, may indeed be specific for depressive disorder (even though exits per se may not). In reviewing the data from Jacobs, Prusoff and Paykel (1974), depressed patients experienced 23 exits versus 4 entrances during the six months prior to onset, while the schizophrenics reported 12 exits compared to 8 entrances during the same period of time. Thus, one might argue that the life change leading to depressive disorder consists of a disproportionate number of exits from the social field as compared to entrances. On the other hand, the life change leading to schizophrenia might be conceptualized as consisting of a rapid turnover among the individuals in one's social field, combining numerous exits and numerous entrances.

In summary, the available evidence from direct comparisons between depressed patients and schizophrenic patients would suggest that, while life events are more strongly associated with depressive disorder than schizophrenia, life events are of some importance in the precipitation of both disorders. The findings point to the need to investigate specific categories of events, rather than events in general, in their influence on the development of specific types of psychiatric disturbance.

THE WORK OF GEORGE W. BROWN

The literature review of this chapter, like that of the last, will close with a detailed discussion of the work of George W. Brown and colleagues, the most recent and perhaps most provocative work in this area. The discussion which follows is essentially an encapsulation of data presented by Brown *et al.* in an article originally published in 1973, and the recent text, *Social Origins of Depression: A Study of Psychiatric Disorder in Women,* by Brown and Harris (1978).

Brown and his colleagues studied 114 women, aged 18 to 65, living in Camberwell, England, who had recently contacted a psychiatrist as an inpatient (73 women) or an outpatient (41 women), with a primary diagnosis of depressive disorder and an onset or exacerbation of depressive symptoms within 12 months prior to entry into the study. They also conducted two random surveys of women aged 18 to 65 living in Camberwell and in this fashion collected a control sample of 458 subjects. These control subjects were personally interviewed. Included in the interview was a modified version of the Present State Examination, a standardized instrument designed to elicit psychiatric symptoms during the preceding year. 76 of the control subjects were identified, on the basis of the Present State Examination, as suffering from recognizable clinical syndromes during the year prior to interview, and will hereafter be referred to as "cases." 68 of these 76 women were identified as suffering a depressive syndrome, and of the 76 women identified as cases during the 3 months prior to interview, 70% could be shown to meet Feighner criteria for depressive disorder. The remaining 382 control subjects who were not identified by the Present State Examination as cases will hereafter be referred to as "normal." Such were the means selected by Brown and his colleagues for the definition of experimental and control groups.

The next methodological step to be considered is the selection of life events to be studied. In marked contrast to the majority of investigators previously cited, Brown rejected the Social Readjustment Rating Scale, or any modification thereof, for this purpose. He argues that the SRRS is excessively vague in its description of life events; for example, one of the items on the scale pertains to "changes in health in a family member." The patient or subject is expected to respond with a "yes" or "no" reply as to whether this particular event has occurred within the recent past. Clearly, an item such as "changes in health in a family member" lends itself to a potentially wide variety of interpretations by the subject; one subject may interpret the item to refer to serious illnesses in immediate family members, while another individual might interpret it to include more trivial illnesses in more distant family members. As a result, the meaning of an event, such as a trivial illness in a distant relative, to the individual subject will influence his or her score on the SRRS. In turn, psychiatric illness or other factors (e.g., anxiety) which influence the meaning of events to an individual will likewise influence his or her score on the SRRS. Thus, if individuals are depressed when administered the SRRS, or if individuals between depressive episodes experience a higher level of anxiety than do normals, their scores on the SRRS may be higher than those of normals as a result of these emotional factors rather than as a result of a true difference in the occurrence of specific life events.

As an alternative to the SRRS (or a modification thereof), Brown and his colleagues collected detailed information from their subjects regarding life events—and considerable biographical material surrounding each life event—occurring during the 12 months prior to admission to treatment for patients, and 12 months prior to interview in the case of control subjects. The investigators developed 28 scales to describe different aspects of each life event, for example, the degree to which the subject expected the event, the amount of prior experience the subject had with similar events, and the amount of support available to the subject at the time of the event. A number of these scales excluded all consideration of what the subject reported she felt in response to the event; these scales were called "contextual scales." These contextual scales were used to judge the likely meaning of a given event to the average person. Events were then included for study if they were judged (by criteria delineated prior to interviewing) to be emotionally important for most people. Events were excluded from further consideration when there was any suggestion that they had been produced by the disorder.

For the first 50 depressed patients, an additional informant was interviewed. There was agreement regarding 79% of the events reported by either the patient or the additional informant in the 12 months prior to onset—a considerable improvement over the 57% rate of agreement between patients and relatives reported by Hudgens, Robins, and Delong (1970). The higher rate of agreement may be related to the fact that Brown and colleagues required no judgement by the patient or informant as to the importance or stressfulness of individual events, as did earlier investigators. There was even higher agreement, 92% agreement, with regard to the occurrence of markedly and moderately threatening events (which will now be defined).

Brown and his colleagues found that the one contextual scale of greatest importance in relating any specific life event with subsequent depressive disorder was that employed to measure an event's threatening implications, i.e., the degree of threat or unpleasantness which would be associated with an event by the average person. Further, events involving long-term threat, i.e., unpleasantness persisting a week or more after the event's occurrence, were found to be of more importance than events involving only short-term threat, i.e., unpleasantness persisting less than one week. (An example of an event involving long-term threat would be a subject's learning of her daughter's many thefts; an example of an event involving only short-term threat would be a subject's delivering a neighbor's baby.)

Unfortunately, it was determined early in the course of the investigation that the inter-rater reliability regarding ratings of the threatening implications of events was only 0.75. In order to reduce that unreliability, each interviewer subsequently read an account of each individual event and the circumstances surrounding that event (without any mention of the subject's reaction or eventual psychiatric status) to the three other investigators, who rated each event independently, and then openly discussed any discrepancies in ratings and ultimately agreed on a rating as a team.

Only events rated as involving a marked long-term threat, and events focused on the subject herself (e.g., an accident involving the subject as opposed to an accident involving a family member or a friend of the subject) and rated as involving moderate long-term threat were found to be reported more often by the depressed patients than controls. These events Brown and his colleagues grouped together under the heading of "severe" events. Three-quarters of these events were found to be independent events, that is, imposed on the subject, beyond the subject's control (and thus not conceivably due to the subject's illness). Three-quarters of the severe events were also found to involve some loss or disappointment, though less than one-tenth of the severe events involved bereavement, i.e., death of a loved one.

Brown and Harris (1978) compared the rate of events reported by patients prior to the onset of their depression to the rate of events reported by normals (excluding cases) prior to interview. Among depressed patients, the onset of depression predated the interview by an average of 14 weeks. Therefore, the analysis of events predating the onset was limited, on the average, to 38 weeks for depressed patients, and so a comparable 38-week period was chosen for analysis of events in the normal control group. Depressed patients reported severe events more than four times as often as did the normals (an average of 1.15 severe events per depressed patient, compared to 0.27 severe events per normal subject). For the same period of time, patients and normals reported non-severe events with virtually identical frequencies (an average of 1.75 non-severe events per depressed patient, compared to 1.91 non-severe events per normal). To look at the same data in a different way, 61% of the patients reported one or more severe events prior to the onset of their illness, while only 20%

of the normals reported a severe event in a comparable period of time ($p < 0.001$). Further, 68% of the cases (women identified by the Present State Examination as suffering a recognizable clinical syndrome during the year prior to interview) reported the occurrence of one or more severe events prior to the onset of their symptoms, compared to 20% of the normals ($p < 0.001$). Brown and his colleagues argue on the basis of these data (and complex mathematical arguments in their text) that severe events exert a formative, or causal, effect in the development of depressive disorder.

Among the 458 women identified in the random surveys of Camberwell (excluding the depressed patients), depression (case-hood) was much more common among working class women than middle class women. This class difference with regard to the incidence of depressive disorder was restricted to women with children; no class difference with regard to the incidence of depressive disorder was found among women without children. Similarly with regard to life events, only severe events demonstrated a class difference (more common among working class than middle class women), and only among women with children.

Yet, this class difference regarding the frequency of severe events did not in itself account for the class difference regarding the risk of depressive disorder. Of the women with children who experienced a severe event (or a severe problem of two or more years' duration, unrelated to health), 31% of the working class women subsequently developed a depressive episode compared to only 8% of the middle class women. Thus, not only did working class women experience severe events more frequently than did middle class women, but working class women were more vulnerable to the development of depressive disorder after a severe event than were middle class women.

The issue of vulnerability has been touched upon earlier in our discussion. Clearly, no given life event produces an identical response in every individual who experiences it. As noted previously (Clayton, 1979), the death of a spouse is commonly associated with the appearance of a depressive syndrome in the surviving partner; nevertheless, while perhaps half of the surviving partners will meet Feighner criteria for depression during the year after their loss, half will not. To extend the same line of reasoning, any other given life event is likely to result in the development of depressive disorder in only a small proportion of those individuals who experience it. Paykel (1974) estimated on the basis of his research (and a rough approximation as to the incidence of depressive disorder in the general population) that only 9.2% of events involving an exit from the social field are followed by depressive disorder in the individual experiencing that loss. Brown and Harris (1978) estimated on the basis of their research that only one in five women who experience a severe event will subsequently develop definite depressive disorder. The question then arises as to what makes certain individuals vulnerable to the development of depressive disorder in the face of provoking life events.

Brown and his colleagues included in their interviews questions regarding persons with whom the subject could talk about things that were troubling her and the quality of her relationships with those individuals. The subject was rated *a* with regard to intimacy if she described a close, intimate, confiding relationship with a husband or boyfriend. She was rated *b* if she described a confiding relationship with someone else whom she saw at least weekly. She was rated *c* or *d* with regard to intimacy if she reported anything less than the above.

Intimacy was found to be a powerful mediator between provoking (severe) events and the subsequent onset of depressive disorder. Of the women interviewed in the random surveys (excluding patients) who were rated *a* on intimacy, only 10% who experienced a severe event (or severe problem of two or more years' duration, unrelated to health) subsequently experienced the onset of a depressive syndrome, compared to 26% of the women rated *b* on intimacy, and 41% of those rated *c*. Thus, intimacy was identified as a vulnerability factor with regard to depressive disorder.

On the basis of their research, Brown and his colleagues identified three additional vulnerability factors: loss of mother prior to age 11 (as discussed in Chapter 4), three or more children under the age of 14 living in the subject's home, and unemployment. Each of these factors significantly increased the likelihood that a woman would develop depressive disorder if exposed to a severe event. Intimacy was found to be by far the most powerful of the vulnerability factors; the existence of a close, intimate, confiding relationship with husband or boyfriend was demonstrated effectively to neutralize the influence of unemployment, for example.

This finding regarding the importance of intimacy in modifying an individual's response to life events is highlighted by Clayton's work with bereaved individuals. Clayton, Halikas, and Maurice described in an article in 1972 their study of 109 randomly selected widows and widowers evaluated by interview one month after the death of their spouses. 35% of their subjects were found to exhibit a reactive depression at the time of interview. The group of bereaved with reactive depression were compared to the group of bereaved with fewer depressive symptoms on 53 demographic, social and physical variables. One social variable clearly differentiated the two groups in that fewer of the bereaved with reactive depression had children whom they considered close in the immediate geographic area. The authors concluded that this difference of support (lack of intimacy) might be thought of as a causative (vulnerability) factor in the development of reactive depression in response to the death of a spouse.

Let us return to the issue of class differences which Brown and associates discovered as regards the occurrence of depressive disorder. Working class women were discovered, in addition to being more likely to experience a severe event, to be more likely to lack a confidante, to have lost their mothers prior to age 11, and to have 3 or more children under age 14 at home. These differences were sufficient to explain (statistically) the class differences with regard to risk of depressive disorder.

It should be noted that the findings we have been discussing with regard to class differences in the risk of depressive disorder—and the discovery of vulnerability factors important in the development of depressive disorder—arose from comparisons between cases and normals. Brown and Harris (1978) were unable to replicate a number of these findings when comparing patients and controls. Specifically, class differences were not replicated, nor were the existence of vulnerability factors of loss of a mother and the presence of young children in the home. In attempting to explain away these discrepancies, Brown and his colleagues suggest that the presence of three or more children under age 14 in the home make contact with a psychiatrist less likely; women with young children in the home may become depressed (cases) but fail to seek out a psychiatrist (become patients) for treatment for their depression. The investigators further suggest that, because loss of mother prior to the age of 11 is statistically correlated with subsequently having three or more children in the home, loss of mother prior to the age of 11 cannot be replicated as a vulnerability factor in a patient population for similar reasons.

Before we summarize Brown's conclusions let us take a brief moment to mention the work of Brown and his colleagues with regard to the association of life events with neurotic as opposed to endogenous depression, and depression as compared to schizophrenia. Brown and Harris (1978) asked a research psychiatrist (who was given no information as to patients' life-event histories) to classify each of their patients (excluding two patients with definite manic symptoms and one patient whose protocol was lost) as either psychotic (62 patients) or neurotic (49 patients) in their manifestation of depressive symptoms. The authors then reviewed these patients' life-event histories and compared the psychotic depressives with neurotic depressives as to their reporting of severe events (or severe problems of 2 or more years' duration, unrelated to health) prior to the onset of their illnesses. 71% of the psychotic patients reported such a severe event (or problem), compared to 80% of the neurotic patients; there was no difference between the two groups.

The authors then took an alternative approach to the same question. They began by classifying patients as to whether they had reported one or more severe events (or problems) prior to the onset of illness (83 patients reported at least one such event or problem, compared to 28 patients who reported none). They then compared these two groups with regard to clinical symptomatology. The clinical differences were few, little more than might be expected by chance, although the differences that were discovered do reflect traditional thinking. Four items (identified on admission to treatment) demonstrated differences between the two groups. Loss of appetite and early morning waking were both more common in the "endogenous" group (the group of patients reporting no severe events or problems prior to onset), while suicide attempts and hopelessness were found to be more common in the "reactive" group.

Brown and Birley reported in 1968 the results of a study of the relationship between life events and the onset of schizophrenia. They administered a standardized interview to a group of patients shortly after their admission to the hospital, patients diagnosed as schizophrenic according to conventional Kraepelinian criteria. Schizophrenic patients were included in the study if the onset of their illness could be dated within 13 weeks of admission. Fifty patients were so selected, each patient interviewed with regard to events during the 13 weeks prior to the onset of his or her illness. To obtain a comparison group, the authors sent a standard letter to a random selection of employees at six local firms. Three hundred twenty-five representatives of the general population were thus selected, each subject subsequently given a similar interview concerning the occurrence of events during the previous three months. Events included for analysis usually involved either danger, significant changes in health, status or way of life, the promise of these, or important fulfillments or disappointments—life events which might be expected to give rise to marked emotions in many people.

The schizophrenic patient group reported nearly twice as many such events as did the general population sample with regard to the 13-week period under study (on the average, 1.74 events per patient, compared to 0.96 events per control; $p < 0.001$). Upon further analysis, it was determined that this difference in the frequency of reported life events between patients and controls was limited to a 3-week period before onset/interview. Sixty percent of the patients had at least one such event in the 3-week period before onset, compared to 19% of the controls during the 3-week period before interview ($p < 0.001$). At the same time, there was no difference in the frequency of life events reported by the two groups prior to that 3-week period. The authors concluded in their original manuscript (Brown and Birley, 1968) that the evidence suggests that environmental factors can precipitate a schizophrenic attack, and that such events tend to cluster in the three weeks prior to onset. Brown and his colleagues subsequently reviewed the data from that initial study, particularly with regard to the threatening implications of the events reported by the schizophrenic patients and the controls. They found that consideration of the degree of threat of events changed the initial results very little; again, differences between the schizophrenic patients and controls were largely restricted to the 3-week period prior to onset (suggesting a triggering, but not a formative effect), and events involving little or no long-term threat were as strongly implicated as precipitants as were more threatening events.

These findings clearly support two of our earlier conclusions. First, research has failed to identify any subtype of depressive disorder which is more likely to be associated with life events than any other depressive subtype. Second, while life events are of importance in the precipitation of both depressive disorder and schizophrenia, certain categories of life events (either a disproportionate number of exits from the social field as compared to entrances, or threatening events) appear to be more strongly associated with depressive disorder than with schizophrenia. Let us now proceed to a discussion of Brown's conclusions regarding the relationship between life events and depressive disorder.

Brown and Harris (1978) concluded (if I may paraphrase them) that certain vulnerability factors (including lack of intimacy, loss of mother prior to age 11, presence of 3 or more children under age 14 in the home, and unemployment) restrict a woman's sense of self-esteem and mastery. Feelings of low self-esteem and lack of mastery, in turn, restrict her ability to develop or maintain an optimistic view regarding her potential to control her world so as to effect restoration when faced with a significant loss. In the face of such a loss (or threatening event), a woman is likely to feel hopeless; the presence of any or all of the vulnerability factors which we have described contribute to a generalization of this hopelessness and, clinically, depression.

PERSONALITY AND DEPRESSION

Numerous attempts have been made to replicate and extend the findings of Brown and Harris of an association between certain social vulnerability factors and depression. Roy (1978) compared a group of depressed female patients with a matched control group of gynecological inpatients and confirmed the findings that loss of mother before 11 years of age, 3 or more children under 14 at home, a lack of a confiding marital relationship, and unemployment are associated with depressive disorder in working-class women. Roy (1978) postulated that personality factors may contribute to these vulnerability factors, especially a lack of intimacy. In a similar, subsequent study (Roy, 1981), the same investigator compared a group of depressed male patients with a matched control group of male orthopedic patients and reported similar findings—that social vulnerability factors (parental loss before 17 years, poor marriage, and unemployment) are associated with depression in men. Again the author commented that many of the depressives were thought to have personality deficits.

A procedural replication of the Camberwell study (Brown and Harris, 1978) was conducted in Calgary, Alberta (Costello, 1982). The Calgary study failed to find an association between social class, employment status, number of children at home, or loss of mother before age 11 and onset of depression in women. The author concluded that the role of these social factors in the onset of depression is community-specific. In agreement with Brown, Costello found lack of intimacy to increase the risk of depression. And, in agreement with Roy (1978), Costello (1982) suggested that lack of intimacy may have its source, at least partly, in the premorbid personality of the individual. Murphy (1982), in her comparison between elderly depressed subjects and normal elderly people in the general population, found that those elderly people who lacked a confiding relationship were more vulnerable to depressive disorder. Like the authors cited above, she argued that such relationships usually reflect life-long personality adjustment, i.e., that personality is a major vulnerability factor in the development of Major Depression (Murphy, 1982).

This assumption, that personality disturbance precedes depressive episodes, has yet to be demonstrated in large-scale, rigorous, prospective research. Previous research into the relationship between personality and depression has been hampered by a number of conceptual and methodologic problems. But Akiskal *et al.* (1983), in a selective review of this literature, conclude that available evidence is strongest for introversion as a possible premorbid trait among primary, unipolar depressives. Preliminary data from the Clinical Studies of the National Institute of Mental Health—Clinical Research Branch Collaborative Program on the Psychobiology of Depression support this conclusion (Hirschfeld *et al.,* 1983).

DISCUSSION

This is a controversial area. Any conclusions are subject to justifiable criticism. Much of the research suffers from flaws in methodology. More recent, more innovative, studies require replication. Given the above qualifications, let me offer my own conclusions.

First, evidence to the effect that unipolar depressive disorder is more likely to be precipitated or caused by life events than Bipolar Disorder is lacking. In the same vein, evidence to the effect that reactive (or neurotic) depression is more likely to be precipitated or caused by life events than endogenous depression is also lacking. Second, evidence that depressive disorder is more likely to be precipitated or caused by life events (in general) than is any other medical or psychiatric disorder has not been established. Third, a growing body of evidence (based on studies comparing depressed patients with schizophrenic patients and with general population controls) suggests that depressive disorder may be precipitated, even caused, by a specific category (or categories) of life events, perhaps best described as those events which involve losses (exits from the social field) or other unpleasantness or threat (undesirable events). Fourth, a growing body of evidence (based on studies comparing depressed patients with general population and medically ill controls, and supported by studies of bereaved individuals) suggests that certain social factors, especially lack of intimacy, increase an individual's vulnerability to development of depressive disorder. Fifth, and finally, available evidence suggests that this lack of intimacy may be due to a lack of capacity for intimacy, or social introversion, a premorbid personality trait of at least some primary, unipolar depressives.

The need for additional research, designed with the methodological considerations I have outlined, is obvious. I will offer some suggestions regarding the direction of that research in Chapter 8. But before we get too far ahead of ourselves, let us stop for a moment and attempt to apply the information presented thus far to the primary prevention of depressive disorder.

REFERENCES

Akiskal, H.S., Hirschfeld, R.M.A., and Yerevanian, B.I.: The relationship of personality to affective disorders: a critical review. *Arch. Gen. Psychiat., 40*:801–810, 1983.

Brown, G.W., and Birley, J.L.T.: Crises and life changes and the onset of schizophrenia. *J. Health Soc. Behav., 9*:203–214, 1968.

Brown, G.W., and Harris, T.: *Social Origins of Depression: A Study of Psychiatric Disorder in Women.* The Free Press, New York, 1978.

Brown, G.W., Sklair, F., Harris, T.O., and Birley, J.L.T.: Life-events and psychiatric disorders—Part I: Some methodological issues. *Psychol. Med., 3*:74–87, 1973.

Clancy, J., Crowe, R., Winokur, G., and Morrison, J.: The Iowa 500: Precipitating factors in schizophrenia and primary affective disorder. *Comp. Psychiat., 14*:197–202, 1973.

Clayton, P.J.: The sequelae and nonsequelae of conjugal bereavement. *Am. J. Psychiat., 136*:1530–1534, 1979.

Clayton, P.J., Halikas, J.A., and Maurice, W.L.: The depression of widowhood. *Brit. J. Psychiat., 120*:71–78, 1972.

Costello, C.G.: Social factors associated with depression: a retrospective community study. *Psychol. Med., 12*:329–339, 1982.

Forrest, A.D., Fraser, R.H., and Priest, R.G.: Environmental factors in depressive illness. *Brit. J. Psychiat., 111*:243–253, 1965.

Hirschfeld, R.M.A., Klerman, G.L., Clayton, P.J., and Keller, M.B.: Personality and depression: empirical findings. *Arch. Gen. Psychiat., 40*: 993–998, 1983.

Holmes, T.H., and Rahe, R.H.: The social readjustment rating scale. *J. Psychosom. Res., 11*:213–218, 1967.

Hudgens, R.W.: Personal catastrophe and depression—a consideration of the subject with respect to medically ill adolescents, and a requiem for retrospective life-event studies. In Dohrenwend, B.S., and Dohrenwend, B.P., Eds., *Stressful Life Events—Their Nature and Effects,* pp. 119–134, John Wiley and Sons, New York, 1974.

Hudgens, R.W., Morrison, J.R., and Barchha, R.G.: Life events and onset of primary affective disorders. *Arch. Gen. Psychiat., 16*:134–135, 1967.

Hudgens, R.W., Robins, E., and Delong, W.B.: The reporting of recent stress in the lives of psychiatric patients. *Brit. J. Psychiat., 117*:635–643, 1970.

Jacobs, S.C., Prusoff, B.A., and Paykel, E.S.: Recent life events in schizophrenia and depression. *Psychol. Med., 4*:444–453, 1974.

Kennedy, S., Thompson R., Stancer, H.C., Roy, A., and Persad, E.: Life events precipitating mania. *Brit. J. Psychiat., 142*:398–403, 1983.

Leff, M.J., Roatch, J.F., and Bunney, W.E., Jr.: Environmental factors preceding the onset of severe depressions. *Psychiatry, 33*:293–311, 1970.

Murphy, E.: Social origins of depression in old age. *Brit. J. Psychiat., 141*: 135–142, 1982.

Paykel, E.S.: Causal relationships between clinical depression and life events. In Barrett, J.E., Ed., *Stress and Mental Disorder,* pp. 71–86, Raven Press, New York, 1979.

Paykel, E.S.: Recent life events and clinical depression. In Gunderson, E.K.E., and Rahe, R.H., Eds., *Life Stress and Illness,* pp. 134–163, Charles C. Thomas, Springfield, Illinois, 1974.

Paykel, E.S., Myers, J.K., Dienelt, M.N., Klerman, G.L., Lindenthal, J.J., and Pepper, M.P.: Life events and depression—a controlled study. *Arch. Gen. Psychiat., 21*:753–760, 1969.

Paykel, E.S., Prusoff, B.A., and Uhlenhuth, E.H.: Scaling of life events. *Arch. Gen. Psychiat., 25*:340–347, 1971.

Perris, C.: A study of bipolar (manic-depressive) and unipolar recurrent depressive psychoses—II. Childhood environment and precipitating factors. *Acta. Psychiat. Scand. Suppl., 194*:45–57, 1966.

Roy, A.: Vulnerability factors and depression in women. *Brit. J. Psychiat., 133*:106–110, 1978.

Roy, A.: Vulnerability factors and depression in men. *Brit. J. Psychiat., 138*:75–77, 1981.

Thomson, K.C., and Hendrie, H.C.: Environmental stress in primary depressive illness. *Arch. Gen. Psychiat., 26*:130–132, 1972.

SUGGESTED FURTHER READING

Brown, G.W., and Harris, T.: Social origins of depression: a reply. *Psychol. Med., 8*:577–588, 1978.

Dohrenwend, B.S., and Dohrenwend, B.P., Eds., *Stressful Life Events and Their Contexts,* Neale Watson Academic Publications, New York, 1981.

Hirschfeld, R.M.A.: Situational depression: validity of the concept. *Brit. J. Psychiat., 139*:297–305, 1981.

Lloyd, C.: Life events and depressive disorder reviewed—II. Events as precipitating factors. *Arch. Gen. Psychiat., 37*:541–548, 1980.

Maddison, D., and Walker, W.L.: Factors affecting the outcome of conjugal bereavement. *Brit. J. Psychiat., 113*:1057–1067, 1967.

Matussek, P., and Feil, W.B.: Personality attributes of depressive patients: results of group comparisons. *Arch. Gen. Psychiat., 40*:783–790, 1983.

Tennant, C., and Bebbington, P.: The social causation of depression: a critique of the work of Brown and his colleagues. *Psychol. Med., 8*: 565–575, 1978.

Chapter 6

PRIMARY PREVENTION OF DEPRESSIVE DISORDER

As noted in Chapter 1, primary prevention is defined as the reduction of the incidence of new cases of a disorder and consists of two essential aspects—the promotion of conditions that produce and reinforce positive health, and specific protection against illness. Let us review the evidence cited thus far regarding potential strategies for the primary prevention of mental disorders, specifically depressive disorder.

PROMOTION OF CONDITIONS WHICH REINFORCE POSITIVE MENTAL HEALTH

It seems reasonable to assume that one's inclination toward or away from mental disorder in adulthood is largely determined during one's childhood, and that efforts designed to prevent mental disorder should rightly focus to a large extent upon promoting conditions during childhood and adolescence that reinforce positive mental health. Efforts designed to teach children the basics of proper nutrition, adequate exercise, effective relaxation, problem-solving skills, and social skills are certainly deserving of praise and will hopefully spare the next generation unnecessary unhappiness. But we must be careful to distinguish between the prevention of unhappiness and the prevention of depressive disorder.

As noted in Chapter 4, attempts to demonstrate an association between a variety of untoward events, including loss of a parent, during childhood with later depressive disorder have been less than convincing. Even if such untoward events could be shown to be associated with subsequent depressive disorder, there is currently little more than theoretical speculation upon which to base potential interventions in order to mitigate against the "depressogenic" effect of such events. For example, if parent loss could be shown to predispose a child to depressive disorder as an adult, would an available parent substitute (for example, through remarriage of the surviving parent within a given period of time) overcome the influence of the initial loss and thus reinforce positive mental health? Answers to such questions are lacking.

The best evidence in favor of the possible efficacy of the promotion of conditions that reinforce positive mental health during adulthood comes from the work of Brown and his colleagues reviewed in Chapter 5. Brown proposes the existence of four vulnerability factors with respect to depressive disorder. The first such factor is the loss of one's mother before one reaches the age of eleven. Suffice it to say that such a loss is as a rule inevitable and that, as noted above, interventions which might minimize its influence as a vulnerability factor are currently hypothetical.

The second vulnerability factor, the presence of three or more children under age 14 in the home, would suggest the desirability of family planning, if not zero population growth. The third vulnerability factor, unemployment, speaks for itself. Few would argue against the many potential benefits from reducing the unemployment rate. The final vulnerability factor, lack of intimacy, seems at first glance more difficult to influence, either at an individual or a societal level, than any of the other three. Conceivably, a school-based program of social skills training for children might increase individuals' (especially, introverted individuals') ability to form and maintain confiding relationships.

On the basis of their studies, Brown and Harris (1978) suggest the need for broad political and social change in order to reduce vulnerability to depressive disorder in the population as a whole. Yet the specific changes to which their conclusions point (family planning and increased employment) have been advocated by others, politicians and sociologists alike, for some time. It seems doubtful, even if numerous other researchers replicate the findings of Brown and associates, that this added impetus toward family planning and increased employment would be likely to have any significant impact. And the physician's role in forging such political and social changes, beyond educating the public with regard to clearly demonstrated "vulnerability factors," is at best uncertain.

With respect to suggestions for the promotion of positive mental health, it seems that scientific investigation has added little to common-sense prescriptions to work and to love (and, perhaps, to bear children in moderation). If we cannot scientifically promote positive mental health, can we not do something to specifically protect ourselves against the occurrence of depressive disorder?

SPECIFIC PROTECTION AGAINST DEPRESSIVE DISORDER

Genetic Counseling (Protection Against Heredity)

If the etiology of Major Depression is at least in part genetic, can we not protect against its occurrence by genetic counseling?

Genetic counseling with respect to any inherited illness depends first and foremost upon accurate diagnosis. With respect to depressive disorder, it is essential in a given patient to distinguish between unipolar and bipolar disorder, and between primary and secondary depressive disorder. Further, effective counseling depends upon a complete and accurate pedigree of the patient's family with respect to the disorder in question, based on family history, or preferably family study (personal interviews with as many family members as possible). Finally, the counselor must be able to provide the patient with information as to the risk of the disorder recurring in subsequent generations and the potential burden of that disorder (severity, occupational and social impairment from the disorder, and the response of the disorder to available treatment).

The mode of transmission of affective disorder from one generation to the next is unknown, with the likely exception of a subgroup of patients with Bipolar Disorder whose illness is transmitted as an X-linked dominant. While, in counseling the bipolar patient, it is thus important to seek in the pedigree evidence for X-linked dominant transmission in order to accurately predict the risk of recurrence in subsequent generations, such families (with bipolar illness and X-linked transmission) are so few compared to the larger group of unipolar and bipolar patients without demonstrable X-linked transmission as to be of little practical import. Almost certainly, affective disorder constitutes a genetically heterogeneous group of disorders with several as yet unidentified modes of transmission from one generation to the next.

Under these circumstances, one must fall back upon empirical morbidity risks regarding the likelihood, given an ill proband (patient), that a first-degree relative will also develop the illness (Kay, 1978). But before we discuss the empirical morbidity risks of unipolar and bipolar disorders among family members of patients with these illnesses, some words of caution are appropriate. Such risk factors are determined by the study of a large number of patients with a given disorder and their families. While the figures are useful in counseling, they cannot be rigorously applied to each family of each patient with affective disorder; a number of additional factors influence the likelihood that an illness is heritable in any given family. For example, the risk that another member in a family of a patient with affective disorder will also be affected by affective disorder may be greater in more severe forms of the illness. Further, evidence suggests that the earlier the age of onset of illness in the proband, the higher the risk that a family member will be similarly affected. Finally, the presence of a family member (in addition to the proband) with affective disorder increases the likelihood that the illness is heritable and, as a result, the morbidity risk for other relatives; in particular, the chance of a patient's sibling falling ill is increased in the presence of an ill parent. As a corollary, the presence of a bipolar relative in the family of a unipolar patient suggests that the familial illness is bipolar in nature and increases the risk of bipolar illness in the patient's offspring. Also, the presence of alcoholism or sociopathy in a male relative of a patient with early-onset depressive disorder (depression spectrum disease) may be regarded as a "depressive equivalent," increasing the likelihood that the illness is heritable and the risk to other relatives.

Given these qualifications, empirical morbidity risks have been derived for patients with bipolar and unipolar disorder and can be considered in determining the likely efficacy of genetic counseling in the primary prevention of affective disorders. Bipolar Disorder affects approximately 1% of the general population, compared to 20% of the first-degree relatives (parents, siblings, and children) of individuals who themselves have Bipolar Disorder. Thus, first-degree relatives (including offspring) of patients with Bipolar Disorder have a twenty-fold increase in the risk that they themselves will suffer Bipolar Disorder.

Primary unipolar affective disorder is much more common, affecting up to 20% of the general population. First-degree relatives of individuals with unipolar disorder have only approximately a two-fold increase in the risk that they will suffer the disorder. In the case of individuals (either patients or their future offspring) with unipolar or bipolar disorder, the frequency and severity of episodes of illness vary considerably, as does response to treatment.

So what can we conclude as to the potential for the primary prevention of depressive disorder via genetic counseling? In drawing our conclusions, it must be noted that the risk that any individual will suffer depressive disorder begins in adolescence and extends throughout the life span; many, if not most, parents whose offspring will later be diagnosed as suffering affective disorder will not themselves have been diagnosed prior to their offspring's birth. Thus, individuals likely to benefit from genetic counseling may well not be able to seek it out until it is too late.

The obvious exception to this rule are individuals with a strong family history of affective disorder in previous successive generations. The identification of family members in more than two successive generations would be more likely in the case of bipolar illness, for which the genetic background of the illness is better established and the increased risk for family members more pronounced. Yet, for the "average" patient with known bipolar disorder, his or her offspring would have an 80% chance of being unaffected by the illness and, if affected, an excellent chance of responding favorably to treatment. Considering the relatively low risk of recurrence in the next generation and the great likelihood of favorable response to therapy in any generation, it seems most unlikely that an individual would choose to remain childless as a result of genetic counseling; we are not currently in a position to effectively prevent affective disorder by genetic counseling.

Prevention of Life Events (Protection Against the Environment)

As noted in the previous chapter, the best evidence that life events are associated with depressive disorder comes from the work of Brown and his colleagues. But even Brown and his associates (1975) express their doubts as to whether measures aimed at the prevention of occurrence of "depressogenic" life events can have more than partial success in that the majority of these events involve losses which are more or less inevitable. They go on to speculate that lack of intimacy (a vulnerability factor which would seem difficult to influence) is likely a better bet in the long term for preventive intervention than most kinds of life events.

Focused Crisis Intervention

If we are unable to protect against the inheritance of a predisposition toward affective disorder, if we are impotent in alleviating social conditions which increase vulnerability to affective disorder, and if we are powerless to prevent the occurrence of undesirable life events which trigger the onset of affective disorder, what is our alternative? One alternative is crisis intervention, intervention to prevent the onset of depression in the face of some undesirable life event.

Directing crisis intervention attempts toward all individuals who have recently experienced an undesirable life event is less than the best use of available resources. After all, only a small minority of individuals develop depressive disorder in response to specific life events. It would seem appropriate to narrow the focus of crisis intervention efforts to those individuals who may be presumed to be particularly prone to the development of depressive disorder in response to undesirable events, i.e., those individuals who, for example, lack intimate relationships, are unemployed, etc. An even more specific approach, an approach which is as yet untested, would be to apply crisis intervention efforts to those persons who have experienced some undesirable event, who are known to be socially vulnerable to the development of depression in response to such an event, and who, in addition, have a familial tendency toward affective disorder.

Two difficulties with such an approach are immediately apparent. First, one must be able to identify this high-risk group in order to have access to these individuals in their time of crisis. Second, one must select the specific intervention (or interventions) to be offered. Two studies of crisis intervention directed toward recently bereaved persons demonstrate both the need for specificity, or focus, in crisis intervention efforts and the potential benefit to be derived from such efforts.

In the first investigation, by Polak and associates (1975), members of a crisis intervention team accompanied a medical examiner of the

Denver County's coroner's office to the homes of families who had experienced a recent death. The first visit usually occurred within 1–2 hours of a family member's death, and the team subsequently met with the family members for 2–6 sessions over a period of 1–10 weeks, employing crisis intervention techniques within a social systems framework. Thirty-nine families received crisis intervention in this fashion and were compared to a control group of 66 families who received no crisis intervention after a recent loss. (Families who had experienced a loss were randomly assigned to the treatment or the control group.) The groups were matched for age, socioeconomic status, education, and residential location. An independent research team collected data regarding a variety of outcome measures, including Beck's Depression Inventory, six months later.

The analysis of the data collected suggests that the crisis intervention program failed to improve family members' coping behavior or to lower the incidence of medical or psychiatric illness or disturbance of social function in the bereaved families. The investigators did note favorable outcome among families who exhibited a high degree of effective communication and those who had available to them an effective network of social resources outside the family. They further noted poor outcome among families who had experienced a loss involving tragic circumstances, e.g., suicide.

These findings point to the importance of controlling for variables related to vulnerability to depressive disorder (in this particular case, lack of intimacy) in such investigations. In addition, the poor outcome of families who had experienced a loss by suicide would be consistent with the hypothesis that the suicide reflected a familial tendency toward depressive disorder which resulted in these families' poor outcome. If nothing else, this study highlights the potential importance of focusing crisis intervention efforts upon high-risk families with genetic loading for affective disorder and without appreciable mutual support.

Raphael (1977) realized that the effects of crisis intervention measures, when directed to the entire population of individuals experiencing bereavement, might be difficult to demonstrate. She thus devised, on the basis of previous research, a series of risk factors to delineate a subgroup of recently bereaved widows at high risk of medical and/or psychiatric morbidity in the near future. These risk factors included a high level of perceived nonsupportiveness (lack of intimacy) in the widow's social network during her crisis, particularly traumatic circumstances of the death (e.g., suicide), and some other concurrent life crisis. Each widow was interviewed, within 7 weeks after her husband's death (after she had contacted the social security department to apply for a widow's pension), with regard to her satisfying the study criteria for high risk of subsequent morbidity. Each widow who was considered to be a member of the high-risk group was then randomly allocated to either the experimental group (n = 31) or the control group (n = 33). Members of the experimental group were seen by the principal investigator for 1–9 sessions (4 on the average), each 2 or more hours in duration. The focus of these sessions was on support of the widow in her expression of grieving affects and facilitation of the mourning process. Crisis intervention sessions were limited to a 3-month period after the husband's death. Follow-up was performed 13 months after the husband's death by way of a general health questionnaire mailed to each subject, with personal follow-up if there was no reply to the initial questionnaire. Follow-up data were gathered regarding 27 widows in the experimental group and 29 in the control group. (There was no difference between the 2 groups with respect to age, years married, religion, number of dependent children, or foreign birth; as the widows were identified by their seeking pensions, they were invariably of lower socioeconomic status. Nor was there a difference between the two groups with respect to the types of risk factors which led to their inclusion in the study.)

Twenty-one of the 31 widows in the crisis intervention group were determined to have a good outcome, compared to only 12 of the 33 members of the control group ($p < 0.02$). This difference in favor of the crisis intervention group was even more pronounced among those widows whose risk factors included a high level of perceived nonsupportiveness; 14 of the 16 experimental subjects with this risk factor experienced a good outcome, compared to only 2 of the 14 control subjects with this risk factor ($p < 0.001$). The author suggests that this particular factor, nonsupportiveness (or lack of intimacy), serves as an accurate predictor of those likely to benefit from this particular form of intervention. It is interesting to note that, of the various outcome variables, depression occurred with more marked severity in the control group than in the experimental group. Four control patients sought medical treatment for depression during the period of study, compared to 3 of the experimental subjects, and 4 of the control subjects required hospitalization for depression, compared to none of those widows who had received crisis intervention.

The first of these two studies failed to demonstrate any benefit from crisis intervention in a bereaved population, whereas the second strongly suggests that crisis intervention may be very beneficial to the bereaved. This rather striking difference in results could be explained by any of a number of differences in design between the two studies. The first offered intervention to various family members, while the second focused only on widows. The first study offered intervention to family members regardless of the circumstances of the death, whereas the second offered intervention only to those whose losses placed them at high risk of subsequent morbidity. And the specific intervention techniques differed in the two studies.

It is difficult not to agree with Raphael (1977) that her ability to demonstrate beneficial effects from crisis intervention is at least in part a result of her focusing on a high-risk group of bereaved individuals. She is to be applauded for her design in this respect. Yet, while her design includes attention to social vulnerability factors, it disregards the potential importance of an hereditary or personal tendency toward affective disorder among the subjects; no mention is made as to the subjects' past or family histories of affective disorder. It is conceivable that the control group could have been, relatively speaking, genetically loaded for depressive disorder when compared to the experimental subjects and that this alone could have accounted for the difference in outcome (at least the marked difference in outcome regarding depressions requiring hospitalization) between the two groups.

CONCLUSION

We are barely beginning to collect the evidence necessary to support and direct efforts toward the primary prevention of depressive disorder. Evidence in favor of attempts to promote conditions within our society which reinforce positive mental health are at best preliminary. More and more researchers are directing their efforts toward identifying within society a subgroup of individuals at high risk (on the basis of heredity, social vulnerability, and recent life events) for the development of depressive disorder. The identification of high-risk factors is not without its methodological nightmares, yet it is becoming more and more apparent that attention needs to be paid to familial predisposition, specific life events, and availability of intimate relationships in this area. Presuming consensus can and will be reached as to the features of a group at high risk with respect to depressive disorder, we are left with the as-yet-unanswered question as to how most appropriately to intervene on their behalf.

To summarize, we are not currently prepared to offer either the public or individual patients primary prevention of depressive disorder. Much additional research must be, and is being, done.

REFERENCES

Brown, G.W., Ni Bhrolchain, M., and Harris, T.: Social class and psychiatric disturbance among women in an urban population. *Sociology 9*: 225–254, 1975.

Brown, G.W., and Harris, T., *Social Origins of Depression—A Study of Psychiatric Disorder in Women.* The Free Press, New York, 1978.

Kay, D.W.K.: Assessment of familial risks in the functional psychoses and their application in genetic counselling. *Brit. J. Psychiat., 133*:385–403, 1978.

Polak, P.R., Egan, D., Vandenbergh, R., and Williams, W.V.: Prevention in mental health: a controlled study. *Am. J. Psychiat., 132*:146–149, 1975.

Raphael, B.: Preventive intervention with the recently bereaved. *Arch. Gen. Psychiat., 34*:1450–1454, 1977.

SUGGESTED FURTHER READING

Crowe, R.R.: Is genetic counselling appropriate for psychiatric illness? In Brady, J.P., and Brodie, H.K.H., Eds., *Controversy in Psychiatry.* W.B. Saunders Co., Philadelphia, 1978.

Lamb, H.R., and Zusman, J.: Primary prevention in perspective. *Am. J. Psychiat., 136*:12–17, 1979.

Tsuang, Ming T.: Genetic counseling for psychiatric patients and their families. *Am. J. Psychiat., 135*:1465–1475, 1978.

Chapter 7

SECONDARY PREVENTION OF DEPRESSIVE DISORDER

Secondary prevention consists of the reduction of the duration of a disorder (and thus its prevalence) through early diagnosis and treatment. First, therefore, secondary prevention relies upon sharp diagnostic methods. With respect to depressive disorder, the DSM–III, with its specific diagnostic criteria, is an organized effort to provide psychiatrists with just these methods. (See Chapter 2 for further discussion.) Second, secondary prevention relies upon effective treatment; the current treatment of depressive disorder is the subject of this chapter. Included in this chapter will be a discussion of current efforts to prevent recurrences of affective disorder (though it may be argued whether such prophylaxis constitutes primary or secondary prevention (see Chapter 1)).

Third, secondary prevention requires an educated public (including the medical profession), a public educated as to the symptoms of Major Depression and the availability of effective treatment. Common clinical experience suggests that a depressed individual, no matter how educated, lacks insight into his illness; the depressed individual is often the last to recognize his own depression. Therefore, we need to educate individuals to recognize symptoms as much in others as in themselves. While efforts to educate the entire population as to the symptoms ("warning signs") of Major Depression deserves serious consideration, an appropriate beginning could be the concentration of such educational efforts upon families of patients with identified affective disorder.

Finally, secondary prevention requires adequate diagnostic and treatment facilities for individuals with affective disorder. In view of the prevalence of depressive disorder (see Chapter 2), not only psychiatrists but family practitioners and internists as well should be prepared to identify and treat Major Depression. Ideally, they should also be able to recognize patients at risk for depression (e.g., individuals who have suffered recent, stressful life events) and educate them as to the symptoms of depression and the availability of treatment. But are physicians prepared to provide these services? A recent study of 58 interns and residents in internal medicinc in a large urban university hospital found that these house officers failed to recognize 34% of psychiatric disturbances, and 76% of recent stressful life events, reported by the patients they interviewed (Brady, 1980). Such findings point to the need for greater emphasis upon the diagnosis and treatment of depressive disorder in the curricula of medical schools and postgraduate training programs in family medicine and internal medicine.

This chapter does not constitute an exhaustive review of the literature (or any part of the literature) with regard to the treatment and prophylaxis of mood disorders. A number of such reviews are readily available to the reader elsewhere. Rather, this chapter offers a selective, and hopefully relevant, look at the current state of the art.

ACUTE THERAPY OF AFFECTIVE DISORDER

When electroconvulsive therapy was introduced in the late 1930's, it was clearly superior to the then-existing modalities (psychotherapy, hydrotherapy, sedation, seclusion, etc.) in the treatment of severe depression (Frankel *et al.,* 1978). Early clinical trials (without the sophistication of control groups or blind evaluation of outcome) enthusiastically reported that electroconvulsive therapy (ECT) led to shortened hospital stays, fuller recovery, and reduced mortality from suicide and other causes. The use of ECT became widespread. ECT became the standard against which drug treatments were measured when introduced in the late 1950's. Even then, comparison studies demonstrated ECT to be at least as effective as antidepressant medications, and in most cases a more effective treatment. Further, ECT was demonstrated to produce improvement in a significant number of patients who failed to respond to antidepressant medications. Additional studies showed that patients suffering vegetative symptoms—changes in appetite or weight, sleep, libido, and psychomotor functions—are particularly likely to respond to electroconvulsive treatments.

Yet, the tricyclics (imipramine, amitriptyline, and their derivatives) were also proven effective in the treatment of severe depression in a series of studies employing placebo control groups and double-blind research design, reviewed by Morris and Beck (1974). And clinical predictors of positive response to the tricyclics (i.e., imipramine and amitriptyline)—including anorexia, weight loss, insomnia, and psychomotor disturbance (Bielski and Friedel, 1976)—were found to be essentially the same symptoms previously demonstrated to be amenable to ECT. Thus both tricyclics and ECT have been demonstrated to be effective in the treatment of severe depression.

Drugs, compared to ECT, are easier to prescribe, less controversial, and more readily accepted by patients. Further, they produce no adverse effect on memory functions, whereas ECT often produces temporary impairment of recent memory. For these reasons, drugs (as a rule, tricyclic antidepressants) have largely replaced ECT as the treatment of first choice for major depressive disorder.

Nevertheless, ECT remains the most effective available treatment for severe depression and is generally considered to produce more rapid clinical improvement than antidepressant medications. Therefore, ECT remains the treatment of first choice of many psychiatrists for patients who are suicidal, homicidal, agitated, debilitated, or stuporous. Electroconvulsive therapy is also the treatment of choice for patients, e.g., the elderly, who are intolerant of medications or unresponsive to drugs, or for whom the drugs pose particular risks (including patients who are immediately post-myocardial infarction or patients who are currently pregnant).

For the remaining majority of patients, tricyclics (in adequate dosage) are effective in abbreviating depressive episodes and reducing associated morbidity and mortality (including non-suicidal deaths, particularly myocardial infarctions (Avery and Winokur, 1976)).

Moreover, current evidence for the efficacy of tricyclics in the treatment of depressive disorder is based upon drug trials employing dosages within a relatively narrow range which were presumed, on the basis of clinical experience, to represent adequate therapeutic amounts. Yet, in the past decade, as determination of blood levels of the tricyclics has become available, it has been demonstrated that individuals vary markedly in their ability to absorb and/or deactivate these compounds; thus, blood levels vary markedly between individuals at any given oral dosage. At the same time, evidence is accumulating which indicates that an individual's clinical response to the drugs is associated with the blood level (as opposed to the oral dosage). As a result, it is conceivable that patients who previously failed to respond to predetermined dosages of tricyclic drugs may have failed because their blood levels were outside therapeutic ranges currently being delineated, and that, with careful monitoring of the tricyclic blood levels, response rates for tricyclics may well be improved.

Furthermore, in the past all antidepressants were considered equally efficacious, and the choice of a drug for a particular patient was based on a prior history of response (when available), a wish to avoid side-effects of certain of the preparations, or simply the individual physician's preference. In the future, however, it may be possible rationally to select a specific tricyclic for an individual patient on the basis of the assessment of a combination of clinical and biochemical variables (Stern *et al.,* 1980). For example, patients with low pretreatment urinary MHPG (3-methoxy-4-hydroxy-phenylglycol) levels plus mood elevation after a single dose of d-amphetamine respond preferentially to imipramine (but not amitriptyline), whereas normal or high MHPG excretion and lack of mood elevation after d-amphetamine are associated with a favorable response to amitriptyline (but not imipramine). The rational selection of antidepressant treatment based on these and additional clinical and biochemical parameters could further improve the likelihood that a given patient will respond to a course of antidepressant medication.

Though electroconvulsive therapy may be as effective in the treatment of mania as it is in the treatment of depression, its efficacy therein has not yet been demonstrated by prospective studies. Lithium, on the other hand, is without doubt effective in the treatment of mania. Doubts remain, however, regarding the value of lithium in the treatment of depressive disorder. Investigations of the use of lithium in the treatment of depression have been reviewed by Mendels (1976), who concludes that there is impressive but not conclusive evidence for an antidepressant effect. Studies demonstrate a clear trend for bipolar depressed patients to respond to lithium more frequently than patients with recurrent unipolar disorder. Thus it would appear that at least a subgroup of depressed individuals may be lithium responders. Nevertheless, at this time tricyclic antidepressants remain the drug of first choice in the treatment of Major Depression.

CONTINUATION THERAPY OF AFFECTIVE DISORDER

Whether a depressed individual is treated with ECT or antidepressant medication, if treatment is discontinued as soon as marked improvement or complete remission is achieved, the patient has approximately a 50% chance of relapsing within the subsequent six months. As a result, continuation therapy—continued use of a therapeutic agent after the disappearance of acute symptoms—has evolved. Its rationale is that somatic therapy (ECT or drugs) suppresses depressive symptoms without substantially altering their underlying pathophysiology, which continues to run its natural course (for an average period of six months per depressive episode).

In the ECT era, a course of electroconvulsive treatments was frequently followed by monthly maintenance treatments to prevent early relapse. Though the efficacy of maintenance ECT's has not been subjected to controlled study, according to a recent survey by the American Psychiatric Association (Frankel *et al.,* 1978), 35% of the psychiatrists currently using ECT in the treatment of depressive disorder also use maintenance ECT's to prevent relapse.

More often, however, tricyclic antidepressants are employed for the continuation therapy of depressive disorder. Continued use of a tricyclic for six months after a favorable response to the drug significantly reduces (i.e., from 50% to 22%) the frequency of relapse during that period (Mindham *et al.,* 1973). Similarly, both tricyclics and lithium have been shown effective (to a similar degree) in reducing the rate of depressive relapse during the six months following a successful course of ECT's (Perry and Tsuang, 1979).

In the future, it may be possible to monitor the pathophysiology which underlies a depressive episode and thereby determine when it has run its course and, accordingly, when continuation therapy can be safely discontinued. As discussed in Chapter 2, most patients with unipolar depression can be identified by abnormalities in their responses to a dexamethasone suppression test (DST) and/or a thyrotropin-releasing hormone (TRH) test. Preliminary studies (referenced in Carroll, 1983) suggest that normalization of these test results indicate a remission of the underlying disorder and predict a decreased likelihood of early relapse. Soon it may be possible to use such laboratory studies as effective guides as to when to start and stop antidepressant medications. For now, we must continue to treat depressed patients employing the guidelines outlined above and a certain unavoidable amount of trial and error.

PROPHYLAXIS OF RECURRENT AFFECTIVE DISORDER

Treatment for a single depressive episode thus lasts six months as a rule. Treatment can thereafter be discontinued. At least it is reasonable to discontinue treatment after six months following a patient's first depressive episode; first-episode depressives have approximately a 50:50 chance of never being depressed (or manic) again in the future. But what about those who suffer recurrent episodes of affective disorder? Can additional episodes of illness be prevented? Is there effective prophylaxis for recurrent affective disorder?

It should be noted that prophylaxis ordinarily connotes complete prevention. This is a misleading connotation in psychiatry today. While a few individuals with known affective disorder have been reported, with prophylactic treatment, to remain free of all symptoms and signs of affective disorder for several years at a time, such a degree of success is not as yet the rule. Prophylaxis more often, and more accurately, is associated with a reduction in the frequency and severity of subsequent episodes of affective disorder. In this latter, more modest sense, prophylaxis remains a most desirable aspect of the overall goal of secondary prevention of affective disorder.

And effective prophylaxis is available, at least for patients with Bipolar Disorder, by way of lithium therapy. Lithium has clearly been demonstrated as effective in reducing the frequency and severity of episodes of Bipolar Disorder (Davis, 1976). Lithium specifically prevents the recurrence of manic episodes in Bipolar Disorder, while its effectiveness in preventing recurrences of depressive episodes remains a matter of some controversy (Quitkin *et al.,* 1976).

Lithium's effectiveness in the prophylaxis of recurrent unipolar depression is even more controversial. John Davis (1976) concludes, on the basis of his review of the available literature, that lithium has significant prophylactic effect (compared either to previous treatment or to placebo) for recurrent depressive disorder. In his opinion, it appears that lithium is equally effective as a prophylactic agent for both unipolar and bipolar disorders. Other psychiatrists seem less convinced of lithium's effectiveness in unipolar disorder, however.

In a special issue of the *Archives of General Psychiatry* entitled, "The Lithium Ion: Impact on Treatment and Research" (July 20, 1979), two recognized experts in the field drew conclusions at variance with one another. On the one hand, Robert Prien remarked that, while results from studies comparing lithium with placebo in a unipolar sample of patients suggest that lithium is effective in reducing recurrences of unipolar depression, the evidence is not as conclusive as with Bipolar Disorder. On the other hand, Mogens Schou, in the adjoining article, concludes that the evidence already available is sufficient to justify the prophylactic use of lithium in unipolar as well as bipolar patients. And so the controversy continues.

While the tricyclics have no place in the prophylaxis of bipolar illness (because they fail to prevent—and sometimes precipitate—manic episodes), they may well have prophylactic efficacy in recurrent unipolar illness. In 1970, the Veterans Administration and the National Institute of Mental Health jointly sponsored a multi-hospital collaborative project including a comparison of imipramine, lithium, and placebo over a two-year period among patients recently hospitalized for recurrent depression (Prien, Klett, and Caffey, 1973). During the fifth to the twenty-fourth month of the study, 29% of the imipramine group and 41% of the lithium group experienced affective episodes, compared to 85% of the placebo group. This evidence is strongly suggestive of a prophylactic effect for both imipramine and lithium in recurrent unipolar affective disorder. The number of patients involved in this study was small, however (n = 56). And the conclusions from this and similar reports are difficult to interpret due to the tendency on various authors' parts, when discussing evidence regarding the effectiveness of lithium and, especially, tricyclics in preventing unipolar illness, to include data from studies of continuation therapy (therapy during the six months immediately following a response to treatment).

In summary, clear and convincing evidence supports the use of lithium in the prevention of recurrent episodes of Bipolar Disorder.

Additional evidence strongly suggests that both lithium and tricyclic antidepressants are effective in the prevention of recurrent episodes of unipolar disorder. While some experts are yet to be completely convinced of these latter findings, both lithium and tricyclic antidepressants are commonly being used as prophylactic agents in unipolar disorder currently.

PSYCHOTHERAPY IN THE TREATMENT OF AFFECTIVE DISORDER

Psychotherapy was the only rational treatment available for depressed patients prior to the introduction of electroconvulsive therapy, and remained the standard treatment of mildly and moderately depressed patients until the introduction of the antidepressant drugs. Initially, the idea of adding drugs to psychotherapy provoked considerable uneasiness with respect to the possibility of negative medication effects (Weissman, 1977). For example, drugs might interfere with psychotherapy by focusing attention only on symptoms as opposed to underlying causes. Medications might increase patients' magical reliance upon the therapist and foster dependency upon the therapist. As a result, the drugs might decrease patients' motivation for active participation in treatment.

During the past decade, however, the overwhelming evidence of the effectiveness of antidepressant drugs in alleviating depressive symptoms has challenged the value of psychotherapy and aroused questions as to the need for psychotherapy in the management of depressive disorder (Weissman, 1977)—especially in view of the relative paucity of evidence for the efficacy of psychotherapy in depressive disorder. After all, psychotherapy could conceivably interfere with drug treatment by increasing patients' anxieties and thus undoing the symptomatic recovery produced by the drugs.

Only recently has research focused on comparing the effects of psychotherapy versus tricyclics (as the current standard treatment of depressive disorder), and determining the relative benefits of a combination of psychotherapy and medications in the treatment of depressive disorder (this research summarized by Myrna Weissman, 1979).

The first controlled, clinical drug trials which included a psychotherapy comparison group were investigations of the effectiveness of tricyclics in continuation therapy of affective disorder. In one such study, the Boston-New Haven Collaborative Depression Project, a group of female outpatients diagnosed as suffering depressive neurosis were initially treated with amitriptyline for four to six weeks. Those whose symptoms responded to amitriptyline were continued on the drug for the next two months. During those two months, one-half of the patients received individual psychotherapy from social case-workers once to twice weekly. This psychotherapy was concerned mainly with current problems, particularly interpersonal relationships with spouse and children, and was supportive as opposed to uncovering in nature. The other one-half of the patients received (as did the psychotherapy group) monthly visits with a psychiatrist for the assessment and prescription of drug treatment. After these two months, one-third of the patients in each group continued amitriptyline, one-third withdrew (on a double-blind basis) to placebo, and one-third withdrew overtly to no medication. All patients continued in therapy, as described (one-half receiving weekly psychotherapy, while one-half received only monthly medication follow-up), for an additional six months of study. The study was designed to include a total of 150 patients (25 patients in each subgroup).

The results of this initial investigation are of some interest. While amitriptyline was demonstrated to have significant effects on patients' symptom ratings during the eight months of continuation therapy, psychotherapy did not (Paykel *et al.,* 1975). Similarly, while amitriptyline had a significant effect in preventing depressive relapse, psychotherapy did not (Klerman *et al.,* 1974). Psychotherapy did, however, show significant effects on measures of social adjustment and interpersonal relationships; these effects took approximately eight months to become apparent (Klerman *et al.,* 1974). There was no evidence from this study for any negative interaction between drugs and psychotherapy; rather, the positive effects from drugs and psychotherapy appeared independent and related to different outcome measures. Thus, the effects would seem to be additive and could be seen as justifying the use of combined treatment in the management of depressive disorder.

Subsequently, the same group studied the effects of psychotherapy (short-term, interpersonal psychotherapy, focused on the social context of the depression), amitriptyline, and combined treatment, versus nonscheduled supportive therapy in the acute treatment of a group of 96 male and female outpatients with the diagnosis of Major Depression according to the Research Diagnostic Criteria. In this second investigation, the symptomatic failure rate was significantly lower in all three active treatment groups than in the nonscheduled treatment group. Also, there were fewer failures with combined treatment (psychotherapy plus amitriptyline) than with either psychotherapy or pharmacotherapy alone; the difference, however, was not statistically significant (Weissman *et al.,* 1979). An additive effect of combined treatment in overall symptom reduction was largely due to differential effects of the two treatments—amitriptyline mainly affected vegetative symptoms (e.g., appetite and sleep disturbance), often as early as the first week, while psychotherapy mainly affected mood, suicidal ideation, interests, and work, often as late as four to eight weeks into treatment (DiMascio *et al.,* 1979).

At one year follow-up of these patients, there were no differential long-term effects of the initially randomized treatment on clinical symptoms; most patients in each of the three treatment groups were asymptomatic (Weissman *et al.,* 1981). While most patients were functioning well at follow-up, patients who had received interpersonal psychotherapy (with or without imipramine) were doing significantly better in social functioning (Weissman *et al.,* 1981).

This study of the effects of psychotherapy in the acute treatment of depressive disorder supports the finding from the same group's earlier investigation of the effects of psychotherapy in the maintenance treatment of depressive disorder—in both cases, psychotherapy produced a positive effect upon social adjustment (or work). The second study suggests, in addition, that psychotherapy has an effect in symptom reduction—a finding not discovered in the initial investigation. This latter result is particularly surprising in view of the fact that the type of psychotherapy employed (interpersonal psychotherapy) did not itself focus upon symptoms or their reduction. A recent study employing a type of psychotherapy which directly focuses upon symptoms and their reduction has produced similar results.

Cognitive therapy has evolved over the past two decades and has recently been applied specifically to depression by Aaron T. Beck (1979). In a test of its effectiveness, Rush *et al.* (1977) compared it to imipramine in the treatment of outpatient depressives. Forty-one outpatients with a diagnosis of unipolar depression (a "definite" depressive syndrome according to Feighner criteria) were randomly assigned to receive either cognitive therapy in twice-weekly hour-long sessions (n = 19) or imipramine with weekly twenty-minute follow-up appointments (n = 22) for a period of study twelve weeks in duration. Both treatments were found to produce statistically significant reduction of depressive symptoms. In comparing the results of the two treatments, there were certain advantages to cognitive therapy. The drop-out rate was significantly higher in the imipramine group (8 patients, compared to only 1 in the cognitive therapy group). And cognitive therapy produced significantly greater improvement on both self-rating and clinical rating scales than did imipramine (even when drop-outs were excluded from data analysis). In all, 78.9% of the cognitive therapy patients showed marked improvement or complete remission of symptoms, versus 22.7% of the imipramine patients (the difference remaining significant even when drop-outs were excluded).

In a twelve-month follow-up of patients who completed therapy in this study, patients from both groups maintained their initial treatment gains. But imipramine patients had twice the cumulative relapse rate of the cognitive therapy patients during the follow-up period, and, at twelve months, the cognitive therapy patients showed significantly lower levels of depression than did the imipramine patients (Kovacs *et al.,* 1981).

The results of this study suggest that a type of psychotherapy, i.e., cognitive therapy, which directly focuses upon depressive symptoms and their reduction, rivals in effectiveness the tricyclic antidepressant drugs in the treatment of mild to moderate depressive disorder. Two subsequent studies have replicated the Rush *et al.* (1977) study and have found cognitive therapy to be at least as effective as tricyclics in similar patient populations (Blackburn *et al.,* 1981; Murphy *et al.,* 1984). Both of these studies included a combined treatment group; neither clearly confirmed the finding of DiMascio *et al.* (1979) of an additive effect between psychotherapy and tricyclic antidepressants in the treatment of depression.

In Chapter 5 I reviewed evidence that lack of intimate relationships predisposes an individual to the development of depressive disorder, and suggested that at least some depressives appear to lack capacity for intimacy. It is generally accepted that social impairment is a common concomitant of depressive episodes, but the findings of a study by Bothwell and Weissman (1977) suggest that social deficits may be a trait, not a state, phenomenon among patients with depressive disorder. These authors assessed 40 women 48 months after their experiencing an acute episode of depression, and found that they were significantly impaired in social functioning when compared to a control group of normal women (Bothwell and Weissman, 1977). These results have been cited as evidence that depressives share a learning deficit in the area of interpersonal skills. A psychoeducational approach—social skills training—has been developed to remedy this deficit through the direct training and practice of such skills.

Bellack *et al.* (1981) have provided the first empirical data on the efficacy of social skills training in the treatment of depression. These authors studied 72 women diagnosed as nonpsychotic, unipolar depressed. Patients were randomly assigned to one of four treatment groups: 1) amitriptyline, 2) social skills training plus amitriptyline, 3) social skills training plus placebo, or 4) time-limited dynamic psychotherapy plus placebo. After 12 weeks, each treatment was decidedly effective and produced substantial improvement in symptoms and social functioning. There was a significant difference across groups in dropout rates, however, with the highest dropout rate (55.6%) in the amitriptyline group, the lowest (15%) in the social skills training plus placebo group. And a significantly larger proportion of patients in the social skills plus placebo group were rated as substantially improved, compared with the other treatment conditions.

Findings from studies of the effects of psychotherapies in the treatment of depressive disorder require replication and extension. Possible variations in future research designs are limited only by the imagination, but should certainly include additional controlled comparisons between each given type of psychotherapy on the one hand and (1) tricyclic antidepressants (with blood level monitoring), (2) combined psychotherapy and tricyclics, and (3) no treatment (or unscheduled supportive treatment) on the other. It would be of interest to include in such studies patients with varied characteristics, e.g., patients who have had multiple episodes of depressive disorder as well as first-episode depressives, and patients who are severely depressed (inpatients) as well as those who are moderately depressed (outpatients). Certainly, long-term follow-up of a large number of patients from such studies will be essential in determining the effectiveness of these techniques in continuation and prophylactic treatment of depressive disorder. And it will be especially interesting to note the effects of psychotherapy among patients who fail to respond to drug treatment.

One can only hope, as Dr. Weissman (1979) anticipates, that the next decade will answer our current questions as to "which type of psychotherapy to use with which drugs, for which depressed patient."

CONCLUSION

Effective secondary prevention of depressive disorder is currently available. Lithium is effective in the treatment of acute mania and in the prophylaxis of Bipolar Disorder. Both electroconvulsive therapy and tricyclic antidepressants are effective in the treatment of Major Depression, and available evidence strongly supports the use of both lithium and tricyclics in the prevention of recurrent episodes of unipolar disorder.

But not every patient is disposed to accept medication as the appropriate treatment for his/her depression. Other patients who accept medication tolerate the side effects of tricyclics poorly if at all. These problems are evidenced by the substantial dropout rates in drug treatment groups in the studies reported by Rush *et al.* (1977) and Bellack *et al.* (1981). For those nonpsychotic, unipolar patients who will not or cannot take antidepressant medication, equally effective psychotherapies—interpersonal therapy, cognitive therapy, and, likely, social skills training—are now available.

While arguments continue to rage as to how best to classify subtypes of depressive disorder, DSM-III currently provides the practitioner with specific diagnostic criteria (for Major Depression) which are known to be related to response to available treatments. Improvement of our attempts toward secondary prevention of depressive disorder must include a concerted effort to educate the public—including physicians—as to these "warning signs" which should lead them to seek—and provide—medical assistance.

But our knowledge with respect to the diagnosis and treatment of depressive disorder certainly will not stop here. The past several years have seen a virtual explosion of information in this area, an explosion which will most certainly continue in the years to come. Potential directions of future research related to the prevention of depressive disorder will be addressed in the next, and final, chapter.

REFERENCES

Avery, D., and Winokur, G.: Mortality in depressed patients treated with electroconvulsive therapy and antidepressants. *Arch. Gen. Psychiat., 33*:1029–1037, 1976.

Beck, A.T., Rush, A.J., Shaw, B.F., and Emery, G.: *Cognitive Therapy of Depression.* The Guilford Press, New York, 1979.

Bellack, A.S., Hersen, M., and Himmelhoch, J.: Social skills training compared with pharmacotherapy and psychotherapy in the treatment of unipolar depression. *Am. J. Psychiat., 138*:1562–1567, 1981.

Bielski, R.J., and Friedel, R.O.: Prediction of tricyclic antidepressant response: a critical review. *Arch. Gen. Psychiat., 33*:1479–1489, 1976.

Blackburn, I.M., Bishop, S., Glen, A.I.M., Whalley, L.J., and Christie, J.E.: The efficacy of cognitive therapy in depression: a treatment trial using cognitive therapy and pharmacotherapy, each alone and in combination. *Brit. J. Psychiat., 139*:181–189, 1981.

Bothwell, S., and Weissman, M.: Social impairment four years after an acute depressive episode. *Am. J. Orthopsychiat., 47*:231–237, 1977.

Brody, D.S.: Physician recognition of behavioral, psychological, and social aspects of medical care. *Arch. Intern. Med., 140*:1286–1289, 1980.

Carroll, B.J.: Biologic markers and treatment response. *J. Clin. Psychiat., 44*:30–40, 1983.

Davis, J.M.: Overview: maintenance therapy in psychiatry: II. Affective disorders. *Am. J. Psychiat., 133*:1–12, 1976.

DiMascio, A., Weissman, M.M., Prusoff, B.A., Neu, C., Zwilling, M., and Klerman, G.L.: Differential symptom reduction by drugs and psychotherapy in acute depression. *Arch. Gen. Psychiat., 36*:1450–1456, 1979.

Frankel, F.H., Bidder, T.G., Fink, M., Mandel, M.R., Small, I.F., Wayne, G.J., Squire, L.R., Dutton, E.N., and Gurel, L.: *Electroconvulsive Therapy.* American Psychiatric Association, Washington, D.C., 1978.

Klerman, G.L., DiMascio, A., Weissman, M., Prusoff, B., and Paykel, E.S.: Treatment of depression by drugs and psychotherapy. *Am. J. Psychiat., 131*:186–191, 1974.

Kovacs, M., Rush, A.J., Beck, A.T., and Hollon, S.D.: Depressed outpatients treated with cognitive therapy or pharmacotherapy: a one-year follow-up. *Arch. Gen. Psychiat., 38*:33–39, 1981.

Mendels, J.: Lithium in the treatment of depression. *Am. J. Psychiat., 133*:373–378, 1976.

Mindham, R.H.S., Howland, C., and Shepherd, M.: An evaluation of continuation therapy with tricyclic antidepressants in depressive illness. *Psychol. Med., 3*:5–17, 1973.

Morris, J.B., and Beck, A.T.: The efficacy of antidepressant drugs: a review of research (1958 to 1972). *Arch. Gen. Psychiat., 30*:667–674, 1974.

Murphy, G.E., Simons, A.D., Wetzel, R.D., and Lustman, P.J.: Cognitive therapy and pharmacotherapy: singly and together in the treatment of depression. *Arch. Gen. Psychiat., 41*:33–41, 1984.

Paykel, E.S., DiMascio, A., Haskell, D., and Prusoff, B.A.: Effects of maintenance amitriptyline and psychotherapy on symptoms of depression. *Psychol. Med., 5*:67–77, 1975.

Perry, P., and Tsuang, M.T.: Treatment of unipolar depression following electroconvulsive therapy. *J. Aff. Dis. 1*:123–129, 1979.

Prien, R.J.: Lithium in the prophylactic treatment of affective disorders. *Arch. Gen. Psychiat., 36*:847–848, 1979.

Prien, R.F., Klett, C.J., and Caffey, E.M., Jr.: Lithium carbonate and imipramine in prevention of affective disorders: a comparison of recurrent affective illness. *Arch. Gen. Psychiat., 29*: 420–425, 1973.

Quitkin, F., Rifkin, A., and Klein, D.F.: Prophylaxis of affective disorders: current status of knowledge. *Arch. Gen. Psychiat., 33*:337–341, 1976.

Rush, A.J., Beck, A.T., Kovacs, M., and Hollon, S.: Comparative efficacy of cognitive therapy and pharmacotherapy in the treatment of depressed outpatients. *Cognitive Therapy and Research, 1*:17–37, 1977.

Schou, M.: Lithium as a prophylactic agent in unipolar affective illness: comparison with cyclic antidepressants. *Arch. Gen. Psychiat., 36*:849–851, 1979.

Stern, S.L., Rush, A.J., and Mendels, J.: Toward a rational pharmacotherapy of depression. *Am. J. Psychiat., 137*:545–552, 1980.

Weissman, M.M.: Drugs and psychotherapy for depression: changing concepts and current evidence. *Current Concepts in Psychiatry, 3*:2–5, 1977.

Weissman, M.M.: The psychological treatment of depression: evidence for the efficacy of psychotherapy alone, in comparison with, and in combination with pharmacotherapy. *Arch. Gen. Psychiat., 36*:1261–1269, 1979.

Weissman, M.M., Klerman, G.L., Prusoff, B.A., Sholomskas, O., and Padian, N.: Depressed outpatients: results one year after treatment with drugs and/or interpersonal psychotherapy. *Arch. Gen. Psychiat., 38*:51–55, 1981.

Weissman, M.M., Prusoff, B.A., DiMascio, A., Neu, C., Goklaney, M., and Klerman, G.L.: The efficacy of drugs and psychotherapy in the treatment of acute depressive episodes. *Am. J. Psychiat., 136*:555–558, 1979.

SUGGESTED FURTHER READING

Klein, D.F., Gittelman, R., Quitkin, F., and Rifkin, A.: *Diagnosis and Drug Treatment of Psychiatric Disorders: Adults and Children,* Second Edition. Williams and Wilkins, Baltimore, 1980.

McLean, P.D., and Hakstian, A.R.: Clinical depression: comparative efficacy of outpatient treatments. *J. Clin. Consult. Psychol., 47*:818–836, 1979.

Paykel, E.S., Ed.: *Handbook of Affective Disorders.* The Guilford Press, New York, 1982.

Rush, A.J., Ed.: *Short-Term Psychotherapies for Depression: Behavioral, Interpersonal, Cognitive, and Psychodynamic Approaches.* The Guilford Press, New York, 1982.

Chapter 8

DIRECTIONS FOR FUTURE RESEARCH

Much must be learned from current and future research in order to make primary prevention of depressive disorder even possible and secondary prevention more effective than it is today. Most of this text has been spent in an examination of past research and an analysis of its deficiencies—a task which is temptingly easy at times. It is more difficult, knowing fully the methodological complexities which plague research in this area, to offer directions for additional research. Yet that is the purpose of this final chapter—to survey the current gaps in our knowledge and to suggest, broadly, the means to filling these gaps. I do not endeavor to offer specific designs for the vast array of investigations yet to be undertaken, but simply offer my encouragement and admiration to the many researchers in various professions who will, no doubt, do so.

FUTURE RESEARCH IN PRIMARY PREVENTION

The Genetic Basis of Depressive Disorder

While research to date has established an important genetic contribution to the etiology of affective disorders, it has identified the mode of transmission of that influence from one generation to the next for only a very few mood-disordered patients (those bipolar patients whose family pedigrees are consistent with X-linkage). The remaining majority of patients are no doubt heterogeneous with respect to their inheritance of a predisposition to affective disorders, and any means of dividing them into subgroups of potential genetic relevance would be most useful. The most promising possibility in this regard is Winokur's division of unipolar disorders into familial pure depressive disease (FPDD), depression spectrum disease (DSD), and sporadic depressive disease (discussed in Chapter 3).

The initial finding by Winokur's group of dexamethasone suppression test abnormalities in the FPDD group, but not the DSD group, must be replicated. And efforts to identify linkage between DSD (or FPDD) and known genetic markers should be continued. To further ascertain the clinical usefulness of this distinction, it would be of considerable interest to compare FPDD and DSD (in studies employing interviews, not chart reviews) as to their association with social vulnerability factors (á la George Brown and associates), personality traits, precipitating (or causal) life events, response to the thyrotropin-releasing hormone test, and response to available treatments.

The dexamethasone suppression test and thyrotropin-releasing hormone test are potentially useful in identifying patients in the midst of a depressive episode and in monitoring the course of that episode (as noted in Chapters 2 and 7). How much more valuable it would be, for preventive purposes, to be able to identify by some laboratory test those individuals with a genetic predisposition to depressive disorder who have not yet become depressed. A research group in the Netherlands, led by van Praag, have reported promising findings in this regard (van Praag, 1979). They demonstrated that a number of patients with depressive disorder exhibit a cerebral deficiency in serotonin, one of the neurotransmitters in the central nervous system—a deficiency which persists even after the abatement of depressive symptoms. They postulate that this central serotonin deficiency is a predisposing factor, a biological expression of a (genetic?) predisposition to depressive disorder. And they have found a higher familial incidence of depression among patients with persistent disorders of central serotonin metabolism than among those without such disorders. Van Praag's studies likewise are in need of replication.

It would be most interesting to compare and contrast those patients with central serotonin deficiency with those without such deficiency with respect to family history (is van Praag's central-serotonin-deficient group the same as Winokur's FPDD?), response to dexamethasone suppression and the thyrotropin-releasing hormone tests, social vulnerability factors, life events, and treatment response (e.g., to antidepressants versus psychotherapy).

Additional candidates for biological markers for genetic vulnerability to depressive illness have been proposed (e.g., Matuzas *et al.*, 1982; Sandler *et al.*, 1983). On the basis of such findings, it may one day be possible to delineate subgroups of mood-disordered patients with known etiology (genetic versus environmental) and predictable response to alternative treatments (biological versus psychological).

The Environmental Basis of Depressive Disorder

At first glance, environment would appear to be of obvious importance in the causation and precipitation of depressive disorder. However, the identification of the specific elements of the environment which cause or precipitate this disorder has proven a formidable task. The sophisticated studies of the social origins of depression by George Brown and his colleagues serve, in most respects, as a model for further investigations in this field.

Future studies must begin by clearly defining the experimental group, by employing a criteria-based definition of depressive disorder, preferably the definition offered by DSM–III. Brown's design, including depressed patients, depressed non-patients, and "well" members of the general population, is worthy of repetition. In addition, a family history (if not a family study) with respect to affective disorder and associated disorders (e.g., alcoholism and sociopathy) should be obtained from each experimental and control subject in order to control, insofar as possible, for genetic influences (and to ascertain whether experimental subjects may be classified as suffering FPDD or DSD, etc.). Ultimately, it would likewise be desirable to obtain from experimental and control subjects those laboratory tests (e.g., dexamethasone suppression tests, measures of central serotonin metabolism) which are developed to confirm the diagnosis of, or even the predisposition toward, depressive disorder. Finally, in order to isolate those social factors important in the formation and/or precipitation of depressive disorder—as opposed to other psychiatric disorders or medical illnesses—studies must be conducted which compare, for example, depressed subjects with schizophrenic subjects or schizophrenic subjects with "normals."

With respect to future research on vulnerability factors, allow me to comment only on what would appear to be the most powerful, most intriguing, and at the same time, most perplexing factor—intimacy. Intimacy, or social support, may act as a buffer between certain stressful life events and subsequent depressive disorder, reducing the likelihood of the latter. But in order to determine whether or not this is the case, valid and reliable measures of intimacy must be developed. Dean and Lin (1977) have reviewed this problem in detail and offer suggestions for its solution as well as proposals for research design regarding "The Stress-Buffering Role of Social Support." I refer the reader to their article for further details.

Research regarding life events and depressive disorder is rapidly increasing in its sophistication and must continue to do so. Investigators must continue to pay strict attention to the demographic composition of each group under study and control demographic variables between study groups (as emphasized by Goldberg and Comstock, 1980). Ideally, groups would also be matched (or at least identified) as to the genetic and biological parameters noted above, accepted social vulnerability factors, and relevant personality traits.

Furthermore, researchers must direct a considerable effort toward a more valid, reliable definition of the life events to be selected for study. The Social Readjustment Rating Scale is unacceptable (for reasons presented in Chapter 5). Nor have any of the various modifications of the SRRS gained widespread acceptance. Brown's approach —determining the degree of threat entailed in a given life event by concensus of the four investigators—was innovative, but painstaking.

At this point it would seem most prudent to focus research on independent events, i.e., events beyond the subject's control, to avoid the possibility that the depression produced the event and not vice-versa. Among independent events, personal losses, or exits from social field, would seem most relevant and most readily and reliably identified. Evidence suggests that additional undesirable (unpleasant, threatening) events may be of importance in the etiology of depressive disorder. Devising an acceptable list of such events is an urgent, though formidable, task. An approach akin to that employed by Paykel, Prusoff, and Uhlenhuth (1971), an attempt to define a scale of life events (each event defined with sufficient precision to require as little interpretation by the subject as possible) and standardize each event as to its relative degree of unpleasantness, seems promising. As previously suggested, such a scale must be validated for groups of varying demographic compositions. An alternative approach, which allows each repondent to rate the direction (positive or negative) and degree of personal impact of selected life experiences, has been reported by Sarason *et al.* (1978).

Finally, assuming that the life events of interest can be identified and defined to everyone's satisfaction, prospective studies are desperately needed. In order to determine the magnitude of risk of subsequent depressive disorder in response to any given event(s) in any given group of individuals, individuals who have just experienced such event(s) must be identified and followed in order to determine how many subsequently become depressed.

Focused Intervention

As noted in Chapter 6, we are today capable of identifying individuals at high risk for the development of depressive disorder in only a very tentative way. In the future, based upon research already outlined, we should be able to delineate such a high-risk group (or groups) with increasing accuracy. As risk factors (e.g., family history, central serotonin deficiency, lack of social support, etc.) are defined, evaluations of prevention programs must certainly control for them. Experimental subjects (those who are offered preventive intervention) and control subjects (those who are not offered such intervention) must be carefully matched with respect to each known risk factor.

But of what shall "preventive intervention" consist? The means of prevention will no doubt be dictated to an extent by the specific risk factor(s) at work in the population under study (and the investigator's area of expertise). For example, if the high-risk group were identified by central serotonin deficiency, the means of prevention might rationally consist of serotonin precursor supplementation. On the other hand, one might choose to intervene in a group of individuals who have experienced personal losses (exits from the social field) by providing, or facilitating their access to, social support. Or, if an investigator believes that depressive disorder is, in the final analysis, a result of depression-prone individuals' irrational belief systems, he or she may choose to offer high-risk individuals training in cognitive restructuring techniques.

Until such risk factors are more convincingly demonstrated, the choice of preventive intervention will remain a matter of guesswork. In the near future, for individuals who have never before experienced a depressive episode (and are not appropriate candidates for tricyclic or lithium prophylaxis), the choice will likely be a form of psychotherapy. But which form? To my mind, whatever form of psychotherapy is selected for study must have one essential attribute—it must be reproducible. That is, different therapists in different places at different times must be able to apply the selected techniques in uniform fashion. Otherwise, variations in preventive efficacy could be simply attributed to variations in technique. Three forms of psychotherapy meet this criteria, cognitive therapy (Beck, 1979), interpersonal psychotherapy, and social skills training (Bellack *et al.,* 1981). All three have been standardized in technique and published in instructional manuals which the interested therapist may employ, step-by-step, in helping clients. (Interpersonal psychotherapy is currently detailed in a manual which may be obtained by writing the Boston-New Haven Collaborative Depression Project*, and will soon be published in text form.) These three forms of therapy appear efficacious in the acute treatment of depressive disorder (see Chapter 7 for a discussion of the evidence) and hold promise as means of prevention.

FUTURE RESEARCH IN SECONDARY PREVENTION

Up to one of every five Americans will, at some point in their lives, suffer a depressive episode. But only a fraction of those who become depressed will seek treatment. Little is currently known about what factors influence a depressed individual toward or away from therapy. Comparisons of depressed patients with depressed individuals who have not sought treatment may eventually reveal the factors which influence patient-hood.

One such factor may be ignorance—ignorance of the symptoms and signs of depressive disorder, and ignorance of the availability of rapidly effective treatment. Primary care physicians must be trained in the recognition and management of mood disorders. The public should be taught as soon as possible to diagnose depression and to immediately seek treatment for depression, once diagnosed, from a physician. (The physician may then confirm the diagnosis, rule out any medical causes for the disorder, e.g., hypothyroidism, and then offer the patient antidepressant medication and/or psychotherapy. The physician may choose to offer psychotherapy him- or herself, or to refer the patient to a more practiced therapist.) In the future, we

*c/o Yale University, Depression Research Unit, New Haven, Conn. 06519.

may be able additionally to educate the public as to risk factors and available methods of prevention—and, perhaps, to employ mass media in preventive efforts (Muñoz *et al.,* 1982). For now, serious consideration should be given to a large-scale effort to inform the public in the diagnosis and availability of treatment for depressive disorder. At the very least, each therapist who sees a depressed individual should make a concerted attempt to teach that individual—and his or her available family members—the symptoms and signs of affective disorder and the importance of seeking treatment early.

Only now is measurement of therapeutic blood levels of antidepressant medications (both tricyclics and monoamine oxidase inhibitors) becoming widely available. In the near future, studies will hopefully document response rates among large groups of depressed patients to these medications with the use of blood-level monitoring. In the more distant future, research may identify specific patient characteristics (e.g., response to a test dose of d-amphetamine) which predict response to a specific somatic treatment—one tricyclic as opposed to another, a tricyclic as opposed to a monoamine oxidase inhibitor, a drug as opposed to ECT, for example. And research may yet succeed in identifying a subgroup of depressed patients who respond preferentially to psychotherapy, eliminating the need for somatic treatment in those individuals.

CONCLUSION

Speaking as a psychiatrist, I consider this an exciting time for psychiatry, particularly for those involved in helping individuals with depressive disorder. We're becoming much more effective in treating this prevalent disorder. And our hope is growing, with good reason, that we may one day be able to prevent such suffering for many. But much remains to be done. We are a long way from effective primary prevention of depressive disorder. Extensive research, along the directions outlined in this chapter, and a lot of luck, may lead us there.

REFERENCES

Beck, A.T., Rush, A.J., Shaw, B.F., and Emery, G.: *Cognitive Therapy of Depression.* The Guilford Press, New York, 1979.

Bellack, A.S., Hersen, M., and Himmelhoch, J.: Social skills training for depression, a treatment manual. *Journal of Selected Abstract Service Catalog of Selected Documents, 11*:36, 1981.

Dean, A., and Lin, N.: The stress-buffering role of social support. *J. Nerv. Ment. Dis., 165*:403–417, 1977.

Goldberg, E.L., and Comstock, G.W.: Epidemiology of life events: frequency in general populations. *Amer. J. of Epidemiology, 111*:736–752, 1980.

Matuzas, W., Meltzer, H.Y., Uhlenhuth, E.H., Glass, R.M., and Tong, C.: Plasma dopamine-beta-hydroxylase in depressed patients. *Biol. Psychiat., 17*:1415–1424, 1982.

Muñoz, R.F., Glish, M., Soo-Hoo, T., and Robertson, J.: The San Francisco mood survey project: preliminary work toward the prevention of depression. *American Journal of Community Psychology, 10*:317–329, 1982.

Paykel, E.S., Prusoff, B.A., and Uhlenhuth, E.H.: Scaling of life events. *Arch. Gen. Psychiat., 25*:340–347, 1971.

Praag, van H.M.: Psychopsychiatry: can psychosocial factors cause psychiatric disorders? *Comp. Psychiat., 20*:215–225, 1979.

Sandler, M., Bonham-Carter, S.M., and Walker, P.L.: Tyramine conjugation deficit as a trait-marker in depression. *Psychopharmacology Bulletin, 19*:501–502, 1983.

Sarason, I.G., Johnson, J.H., and Siegel, J.M.: Assessing the impact of life changes: development of the Life Experiences Survey. *J. Consult. Clin. Psychol., 46*:932–946, 1978.

SUGGESTED FURTHER READING

Andrews, G., Tennant, C., Hewson, D.M., and Vaillant, G.E.: Life event stress, social support, coping style, and risk of psychological impairment. *J. Nerv. Ment. Dis., 166*:307–316, 1978.

Aneshensel, C.S., and Stone, J.D.: Stress and depression: a test of the buffering model of social support. *Arch. Gen. Psychiat., 39*:1392–1396, 1982.

Hirschfeld, R.M.A., and Cross, C.K.: Epidemiology of affective disorders: psychosocial risk factors. *Arch. Gen. Psychiat., 39*:35–46, 1982.

Hirschfeld, R.M.A., Koslow, S.H., and Kupfer, D.J.: The clinical utility of the dexamethasone suppression test in psychiatry. *J.A.M.A., 250*: 2172–2174, 1983.

Mitchell, R.E., Billings, A.G., and Moos, R.H.: Social support and well-being: implications for prevention programs. *Journal of Primary Prevention, 3*:77–98, 1982.

Praag, van H.M.: The significance of biological factors in the diagnosis of depressions: I biochemical variables. *Comp. Psychiat., 23*:124–135, 1982.

Rahe, R.H., and Arthur, R.J.: Life change and illness studies: past history and future directions. *J. Human Stress (March)*:3–15, 1978.

AUTHORS INDEX

SUBJECT INDEX

D

E

U

V

W